THE MEASUREMENT OF ATTITUDE

THE MEASUREMENT
OF ATTITUDE

*A Psychophysical Method and Some Experiments
with a Scale for Measuring Attitude
toward the Church*

By

L. L. THURSTONE

AND

E. J. CHAVE

THE UNIVERSITY OF CHICAGO PRESS

CHICAGO AND LONDON

THE UNIVERSITY OF CHICAGO PRESS, CHICAGO & LONDON
The University of Toronto Press, Toronto 5, Canada

PREFACE

The experiments described in this monograph have been conducted jointly by the two authors. The material for the scale and all the data were compiled by Mr. Chave who made all arrangements for conducting the experimental tests. He was also responsible for supervising the tabulation of the results and he has written chapter vi on "Further Studies of Validity." The chapters on measurement theory were written by Mr. Thurstone, who is also responsible for the statistical methods used.

We wish to acknowledge the assistance of instructors and students who have served as subjects for these experiments by filling in the various forms and by sorting the lists of statements of opinion in various ways. Dean Boucher made it possible to conduct one form of the tests in a Freshman assembly in Mandel Hall and Mr. Fred Moore arranged for conducting a similar test at the Chicago Forum. Dean Shailer Mathews and Professor T. G. Soares placed at our disposal certain funds for the experimental and statistical work, and the Local Community Research Committee at the University of Chicago has also sponsored the project financially. Professor Faris has kindly consented to let us reprint sections of an article in the *American Journal of Sociology* (January, 1928) which described the possibility of measuring attitude. The studies there described were begun under the auspices of the Institute for Juvenile Research. We also wish to express our appreciation of the competent statistical work of Miss Annette McBroom and Mr. C. W. Brown who have been responsible for the statistical work on this monograph.

We regard the present experiments as preliminary in character, and a second scale for measuring attitude toward the church is now in process of construction. It is hoped that it will be relatively free from the defects which we have found in the present experimental scale. Our main contribution is probably in the idea of using the equally-often-noticed difference or, preferably, the discriminal error as a unit of measurement for the objective description of attitude and opinion.

E. J. CHAVE
L. L. THURSTONE

UNIVERSITY OF CHICAGO·
April, 1928

TABLE OF CONTENTS

MEASUREMENT IN RELIGIOUS EDUCATION

In the processes of religious education one of the most significant factors to be considered is the development or modification of attitudes. The goals of modern religious education do not simply involve the attainment of certain bodies of knowledge, such as the Bible, creeds, and doctrinal statements, history of religions, and other records of religious experience but are more closely related to the actual behavior of persons in society. To measure the amount of knowledge that any pupil may have received is fairly easy. The techniques for this kind of measurement are well established and it only requires a careful selection of materials to construct satisfactory tests. The more important concern of religious educators today is to measure how far habits of conduct that are in accordance with modern religious ideas have been established and how far attitudes and values that express the religious tendencies considered to be directed toward the realization of the highest good for the individuals themselves and for the society of which they are members have been developed in individuals and in groups of persons. These attitudes involve tendencies toward the institutions of religion—its symbols, its literature, its expressed doctrines, its concepts, ideals, programs, and other phases of religious living. The attitudes taken by persons indicate the values discovered in their personal and social religious experience.

Religious educators have been for many years changing and rechanging their methods and materials in their desire to promote satisfactory religious habits, attitudes, and values in children, youth, and adults. But as in the field of general education, this revision has been largely dependent upon guesswork and hopeful estimates as to what the results have been and might be. If the results could be measured more accurately the processes of religious eduçation could be more intelligently directed and the desired effects upon character would be more effectively produced. Even the rough measuring tools that have so far been developed have aided in the evaluation of methods. Real progress must wait on the development of more accurate and refined objective measuring instruments.

Religious education is also interested in all social attitudes. In so far as a person has an attitude that is in the direction of the life-goals approved by religious standards, religious education seeks to develop and motivate such with religious faith, purpose, and passion. In so far as the expression of any social attitude may reveal a life set in a direction not approved by religious standards, religious education seeks to change the tendency and redirect the life toward the more ideal religious goal. Thus the measurement of attitudes is a distinct field of interest for religious educators. This study and experiment recorded herein have been undertaken with the recognition of urgent necessity for better tools for obtaining more accurate data regarding the existing and changing attitudes in the individuals and groups with which religious education works.

E. J. CHAVE

SUMMARY OF THE MEASUREMENT METHOD

We have tried to devise a method whereby the distribution of attitude of a group on a specified issue may be represented in the form of a frequency distribution. The base line represents ideally the whole range of attitudes from those at one end who are most strongly in favor of the issue to those at the other end of the scale who are as strongly against it. Somewhere between the two extremes on the base line will be a neutral zone representing indifferent attitudes on the issue in question. The ordinates of the frequency distribution represent the relative popularity of each attitude.

This measurement problem has the limitation which is common to all measurement, namely, that one can measure only such attributes as can be represented on a linear continuum, such attributes as volume, price, length, area, excellence, beauty, and so on. For the present problem we are limited to those aspects of attitudes for which one can compare individuals by the "more and less" type of judgment. For example, we say understandingly that one man is more in favor of prohibition than another, more strongly in favor of the League of Nations than another, more militaristic than some other, more religious than another. The measurement is effected by the indorsement or rejection of statements of opinion.

The opinions are allocated to different positions on the base line in accordance with the attitudes which they express. The ordinates of the frequency distribution are determined by the frequency with which each of the scaled opinions is indorsed. The center of the whole problem lies in the definition of a unit of measurement for the base line. The scale is so constructed that two opinions separated by a unit distance on the base line seem to differ as much in the attitude variable involved as any other two opinions on the scale which are also separated by a unit distance. This is the main idea of the present scale construction.

The true allocation of an individual to a position on an attitude scale is an abstraction, just as the true length of a chalk line, or the true temperature of a room, or the true spelling ability of a child is an abstraction. We estimate the true length of a line, the true temperature of a room, or the true spelling ability of a child by means of various indices, and it is a commonplace in measurement that all indices do not agree exactly. In allocating an individual to a point on the attitude continuum we may use various indices, such as the opinions that he indorses, his overt acts, and his past history, and it is to be expected that discrepancies will appear as the "true" attitude of the individual is estimated by different indices. The present study is concerned with the allocation of individuals along an attitude continuum based on the opinions that they accept or reject.

We are not at all sure that the method we have used is theoretically correct or that it is the best psychophysical method of measuring attitude. It is possible that the method of equal-appearing intervals that we have used in these experiments may be superseded by better psychophysical methods. Our main purpose will have been achieved, however, if we succeed in directing attention to the possibility of measuring attitude as a psychophysical problem. In doing so we are but extending the pioneer work of Cattell, who was the first to apply psychophysical methods to the measurement of social values.

L. L. THURSTONE

CHAPTER I
THEORY OF ATTITUDE MEASUREMENT
THE OBJECTIVE DESCRIPTION OF ATTITUDE

The scientific study of social phenomena suffers from the serious handicap that the phenomena that we call social are exceedingly difficult to describe in objective terms, to say nothing of quantitative measurement. Whenever objective or quantitative treatment is attempted we not infrequently feel that the very essence has been squeezed out of the effects that we want to study. About this feeling concerning quantitative treatment in the social studies two comments may be made. In the first place, when we find those aspects of a social phenomenon which lend themselves to objective and simple counting, it frequently does happen that these things that can be counted are really not essential aspects of the social phenomenon under consideration. But, further, there is also the possibility that as soon as some intriguing problem of social conduct becomes accessible to measurement we are inclined to turn our attention away as though elsewhere must reside the essence of that which we regard as vital, human, or important. This is really a bad habit.

Since the application of psychophysical methods to the measurement of social attitudes contains a certain degree of novelty, it may be appropriate to review briefly the setting in which the present experiments have grown. The psychophysical methods were developed primarily for the purpose of measuring discriminatory powers with special regard to simple sensory stimuli. The classical psychophysical experiments were devoted to the measurement of the subject's power to discriminate between lines of slightly different length, between slightly different weights that he lifted, between pairs of gray papers that differed slightly in brightness, and so on. In experiments of this kind were discovered Weber's law and Fechner's law.

Cattell seems to be the first to have extended the psychophysical methods to stimuli other than simple sensory values. He applied the psychophysical procedures with some variations to the measurement of estimated degrees of eminence of scientific men. Here, for the first time, the methods were used on stimuli which do not have any simple stimulus magnitude. When the methods are used on lifted weights, line lengths, and brightnesses, the experiments yield two scales. One is a scale of physical stimulus magnitude such as the actual weight in grams, the length of the lines in centimeters, or the photometrically determined brightness of the gray papers. It is known in psychophysics as the R-scale. The second scale is the psychological continuum, which is known as the S-scale. Its unit is the equally often noticed stimulus difference. Fechner's law describes the logarithmic relation between these two scales. Weber's law describes the average error of perception as a constant fraction of the physical stimulus magnitude. When Cattell extended the use of these methods to social stimuli he constructed, in effect, a psychological scale, the unit of measurement for which was the equally often noticed difference or some approximation to it.

But when the methods are used for measuring social values there is no simple physical stimulus value to be measured such as line length or weight. The validity of the psychological scale of equally often noticed differences must be established by other criteria of internal consistency. Cattell's students have applied the same methods with variations and short cuts to the measurement of other social values, examples of which are the experiments of Wells in measuring literary merit and the experiments of Thorndike in measuring the estimated excellence of handwriting and of children's drawings. The idea underlying such measurement is the equally often noticed difference, properly defined, as a unit of measurement. In all of these measurements, however, there is no simple physical stimulus scale with which to match the psychological scale. Hence in these experiments the verification of Fechner's law is not an issue.

The last twenty years have witnessed a most peculiar separation into two groups of the men primarily interested in psychological measurement. One of these groups concern themselves with traditional psychophysics with primary emphasis on simple sensory stimuli. They are the psychophysicists. They have developed the psychophysical methods with considerable refinement, inspired by an interest in psychological measurement theory. The other group has proceeded with the construction of educational scales with little or no interest in the available psychophysical methods or their underlying theory. As a consequence there is at present a wide but artificial break between the group of men who work in psychophysics with the traditional stimuli and those who attempt to measure educational and social values with little interest in psychophysical theory. The present study is one of a series of experiments intended to continue the work of Cattell in applying the psychophysical methods to the measurement of social values. It is our hope again to unify the efforts to measure social values with the advancement in psychophysical theory.

We have used the method of equal-appearing intervals for the construction of our scale of attitude. There is some question about the validity of this method since the scale so produced may not be entirely consistent with the scale that would be produced by the method of paired comparison or Cattell's order of merit (rank order) procedure. We leave it for separate experimentation, however, to ascertain to what extent the psychological scales differ when they are produced by the several psychophysical methods.

Before proceeding to describe our experiments and the terminology and methods that are involved, it may be in order to describe first the ultimate purposes of the measuring tools that we are here attempting to develop. What might such a tool be used for? Perhaps such a question is better answered after a more detailed description of our procedures, but it will be discussed here in order to give as practical a slant as may be possible to the experiments that we have undertaken.

Assume that we want to know which form of appeal is most effective for making people change their minds about a disputed issue such as pacifism, prohibition, municipal ownership, birth control, feminism, on which people differ both as regards the actual convictions which they more or less frankly declare and also as regards the emotional load with which the convictions are adhered to. Would it be more effective to make an appeal to a specified kind of audience by presenting facts in favor of one side of the issue or to present an emotional or oratorical address on the subject? The outcome would supposedly differ with the kind of audience on which the experiment was performed.

If we really want to answer such a question with any particular specifications as to the issue, the two types of appeal to be evaluated, the education, sex, and occupation of the audience, and so on, we should want to evaluate first the distribution of attitudes in our audience before the appeal is made, and then evaluate it after the appeal has been made. A comparison between the distributions of attitudes before and after the presentation of the lecture or reading matter would constitute the natural basis on which we should decide as to which of the two types of appeal would be the more effective in making these people change their minds. But how shall the distribution of attitudes or opinions be measured? That is the main problem of the present investigation.

Another situation that arises frequently enough is that of comparing two groups of people in different localities as to just how strongly they feel on some disputed issue. Of course it is possible merely to present a simple proposition on which the two groups vote "yes" or "no," and the total votes on the single proposition would indicate in a simple but crude way how the two groups feel about the question. But such a total vote does not indicate the relative frequency of extreme convictions either for or against the proposition in the two groups, nor does it indicate just how a proposition might be presented in order to command a majority acceptance. If we had a graded series of propositions ranging from one extreme of the issue to the other, then we could present the whole list to the two groups for separate indorsement of each proposition. This is not suggested for popular elections in which the present study has no immediate concern.

On the basis of the resulting tabulations it might be desirable to make a comparison of the two groups by saying that on the average one of them was more strongly in favor of the proposition than the other. But what is the average of the indorsements of a list of propositions? That question could be answered only if the graded propositions could be assigned to a linear continuum of some sort. Then it would be possible to locate the central tendency of the frequency distributions of attitude in the groups, and thereby to compare them by a single index. In the same manner the two groups could be compared as to the dispersions of attitude which they represented only in case a measure of dispersion could be applied to the votes on the list of propositions. A linear continuum is requisite also for the solution of this problem. Our main problem here concerns the possibility of measuring attitudes in such a manner.

THE POSSIBILITY OF MEASURING ATTITUDE[1]

The very fact that one offers a solution to a problem so complex as that of measuring differences of attitude on disputed social issues makes it evident from the start that the solution is more or less restricted in nature and that it applies only under certain assumptions that will, however, be described. In devising a method of measuring attitude we have tried to get along with the fewest possible restrictions because sometimes one is tempted to disre-

[1] Sections of this monograph are reprinted, with permission of the editors, from L. L. Thurstone, "Attitudes Can Be Measured," *American Journal of Sociology*, January, 1928.

gard so many factors that the original problem disappears. We trust that we shall not be accused of throwing out the baby with its bath.

In promising to measure attitudes we shall make several common-sense assumptions that will be stated here at the outset so that subsequent discussion may not be fogged by confusion regarding them. If the reader is unwilling to grant these assumptions, then we shall have nothing to offer him. If they are granted, we can proceed with some measuring methods that ought to yield interesting results.

It is necessary to state at the very outset just what we shall here mean by the terms "attitude" and "opinion." This is all the more necessary because the natural first impression about these two concepts is that they are not amenable to measurement in any real sense. It will be conceded at the outset that an attitude is a complex affair which cannot be wholly described by any single numerical index. For the problem of measurement this statement is analogous to the observation that an ordinary table is a complex affair which cannot be wholly described by any single numerical index. So is a man such a complexity which cannot be wholly represented by a single index. Nevertheless we do not hesitate to say that we measure the table. The context usually implies what it is about the table that we propose to measure. We say without hesitation that we measure a man when we take some anthropometric measurements of him. The context may well imply without explicit declaration what aspect of the man we are measuring, his cephalic index, his height, or weight, or what not. Just in the same sense we shall say here that we are measuring attitudes. We shall state or imply by the context the aspect of people's attitudes that we are measuring. The point is that it is just as legitimate to say that we are measuring attitudes as it is to say that we are measuring tables or men.

The concept "attitude" will be used here to denote the sum-total of a man's inclinations and feelings, prejudice or bias, preconceived notions, ideas, fears, threats, and convictions about any specific topic. Thus a man's attitude about pacifism means here all that he feels and thinks about peace and war. It is admittedly a subjective and personal affair.

The concept "opinion" will here mean a verbal expression of attitude. If a man said that we made a mistake in entering the war against Germany, that statement would be called his opinion. The term "opinion" will be restricted to verbal expression. But it is an expression of what? It expresses an attitude, supposedly. There should be no difficulty in understanding this use of the two terms. The verbal expression is the *opinion*. Our interpretation of such an expressed opinion would be that the man's *attitude* is pro-German. An opinion symbolizes an attitude.

Our next point concerns what it is that we want to measure. When a man says that we made a mistake in entering the war with Germany, the thing that interests us is not really the string of words as such or even the immediate meaning of the sentence merely as it stands, but rather the attitude of the speaker, the thoughts and feelings of the man about the United States, and the war, and Germany. It is the attitude that really interests us. The opinion has interest only in so far as we interpret it as a symbol of attitude. It is therefore something about attitudes that we want to measure. We shall use opinions as the means for measuring attitudes.

There comes to mind the uncertainty of using an opinion as an index of attitude. The man may be a liar. If he is not intentionally misrepresenting his real attitude on a disputed question, he may nevertheless modify the expression of it for reasons of courtesy, especially in those situations in which frank expression of attitude may not be well received. This has led to the suggestion that a man's action is a safer index of his attitude than what he says. But his actions may also be distortions of his attitude. A politician extends friendship and hospitality in overt action while hiding an attitude that he expresses more truthfully to an intimate friend. Neither his opinions nor his overt acts constitute in any sense an infallible guide to the subjective inclinations and preferences that constitute his attitude. Therefore we must remain content to use opinions or other forms of action merely as indices of attitude. It must be recognized that there is a discrepancy, some error of measurement as it were, between the opinion or overt action that we use as an index and the attitude that we infer from such an index.

But this discrepancy between the index and "truth" is universal. When you want to know the temperature of your room, you look at the thermometer and use its reading as an index of temperature just as though there were no error in the index and just as though there were a single temperature reading which is the "correct" one for the room. If it is desired to ascertain the volume of a glass paperweight, the volume is postulated as an attribute of the piece of glass, even though volume is an abstraction. The volume is measured indirectly by noting the dimensions of the glass or by immersing it in water to see how much water it displaces. These two procedures give two indices which may not agree exactly. In almost every situation involving measurement there is postulated an abstract continuum such as volume or temperature, and the allocation of the thing measured to that continuum is accomplished usually by indirect means through one or more indices. Truth is inferred only from the relative consistency of the several indices, since it is never directly known. We are dealing with the same type of situation in attempting to measure attitude. We must postulate an attitude variable which is like practically all other measurable attributes in the nature of an abstract continuum, and we must find one or more indices which will satisfy us to the extent that they are internally consistent.

In the present study we shall measure the subject's attitude as expressed by the acceptance or rejection of opinions. But we shall not thereby imply that he will necessarily *act* in accordance with the opinions that he has indorsed. Let this limitation be clear.

The measurement of attitudes expressed by a man's opinions does not necessarily mean the prediction of what he will do. If his expressed opinions and his actions are inconsistent, that does not concern us now, because we are not setting out to predict overt conduct. We shall assume that it is of interest to know what people *say* that they believe even if their conduct turns out to be inconsistent with their professed opinions. Even if they are intentionally distorting their attitudes, we are measuring at least the attitude which they are trying to make people believe that they have.

We take for granted that people's attitudes are subject to change. When we have measured a man's attitude on any issue such as pacifism, we shall not declare such a measurement to be in any sense an enduring or constitutional constant. His attitude may change, of course, from one day to the next, and it is our task to measure such changes, whether they be due to unknown causes or to the presence of some known persuasive factor, such as the reading of a discourse on the issue in question. However, such fluctuations may also be attributed in part to error in the measurements themselves. In order to isolate the errors of the measurement instrument from actual fluctuations in attitude, we must calculate the standard error of measurement of the scale itself, and this can be accomplished by methods already well known in mental measurement.

We shall assume that an attitude scale is used only in those situations in which one may reasonably expect people to tell the truth about their convictions or opinions. If a denominational school were to submit to its students a scale of attitudes about the church, one might find that some students hesitate to make known their convictions if they deviate from the orthodox beliefs of their school. At least, the findings could be challenged if the situation in which attitudes were expressed contained pressure or implied threat bearing directly on the attitude to be measured. Similarly, it would be difficult to discover attitudes on sex liberty by a written questionnaire, because of the well-nigh universal pressure to conceal such attitudes when they deviate from supposed conventions. It is assumed that attitude scales will be used only in those situations that offer a minimum of pressure on the attitude to be measured. Such situations are common enough.

All that we can do with an attitude scale is to measure the attitude actually expressed with the full realization that the subject may be consciously hiding his true attitude or that the social pressure of the situation has made him really believe what he expresses. This is a matter for interpretation. It is probably worth while to measure an attitude expressed by opinions. It is another problem to interpret in each case the extent to which the subjects have expressed what they really believe. All that we can do is to minimize as far as possible the conditions that prevent our subjects from telling the truth, or else to adjust our interpretations accordingly.

When we discuss opinions, about prohibition for example, we quickly find that these opinions are multidimensional, that they cannot all be represented in a linear continuum. The various opinions cannot be completely described merely as "more" or "less." They scatter in many dimensions, but the very idea of measurement implies a linear continuum of some sort such as length, price, volume, weight, age. When the idea of measurement is applied to scholastic achievement, for example, it is necessary to force the qualitative variations into a scholastic linear scale of some kind. We judge in a similar way qualities such as mechanical skill, the excellence of handwriting, and the amount of a man's education, as though these traits were strung out along a single scale, although they are, of course, in reality scattered in many dimensions. As a matter of fact, we get along quite well with the concept of a linear scale in describing traits even so qualitative as education, social and economic status, or beauty. A scale or linear continuum is implied when we say that a man has more education than another, or that a woman is more beautiful than another, even though, if pressed, we admit that perhaps the pair involved in each of the comparisons have little in common. It is clear that the linear continuum which is implied in a "more and less" judgment may be conceptual, that it does not necessarily have the physical existence of a yardstick.

And so it is also with attitudes. We do not hesitate to compare them by the "more and less" type of judgment. We say about a man, for example, that he is more in favor of prohibition than some other, and the judgment conveys its meaning very well with the implication of a linear scale along which people or opinions might be allocated.

THE ATTITUDE VARIABLE

The first restriction on the problem of measuring attitudes is to specify an attitude variable and to limit the measurement to that. An example will make this clear. Let us consider the prohibition question and let us take as the attitude variable the degree of restriction that should be imposed on individual liberty in the consumption of alcohol. This degree of restriction can be thought of as a continuum ranging from complete and absolute freedom or license to equally complete and absolute restriction, and it would of course include neutral and indifferent attitudes.

In collecting samples from which to construct a scale we might ask a hundred individuals to write out their opinions about prohibition. Among these we might find one which expresses the belief that prohibition has increased the use of tobacco. Surely this is an opinion concerning prohibition, but it would not be at all serviceable for measuring the particular attitude variable on prohibition mentioned in the foregoing. Hence it would be irrelevant. Another man might express the opinion that prohibition has eliminated an important source of government revenue. This is also an opinion concerning prohibition, but it would not belong to the particular attitude variable that we have set out to measure or scale. It is preferable to use an objective and experimental criterion for the elimination of opinions that do not belong on the specified continuum to be measured, and we believe that such a criterion is available.

This restriction on the problem of measuring attitudes is necessary in the very nature of measurement. It is taken for granted in all ordinary measurement, and it must be clear that it applies also to measurement in a field in which the multidimensional characteristics have not yet been so clearly isolated. For example, it would be almost ridiculous to call attention to the fact that a table cannot be measured unless one states or implies what it is about the table that is to be measured; its height, its cost, or beauty, or degree of appropriateness, or the length of time required to make it. The context usually makes this restriction on measurement. When the notion of measurement is applied to so complex a phenomenon as opinions and attitudes, we must here also restrict ourselves to some specified or implied continuum along which the measurement is to take place.

In specifying the attitude variable, the first requirement is that it should be so stated that one can speak of it in terms of "more" and "less," as, for example, when we compare the attitudes of people by saying that one of them is more pacifistic, more in favor of prohibition, more strongly in favor of capital punishment, or more religious than some other person.

Figure 1 represents an attitude variable, militarism-pacifism, with a neutral zone. A person who usually talks in favor of preparedness, for example, would be represented somewhere to the right of the neutral zone. A person who is more interested in disarmament would be represented somewhere to the left of the neutral zone. It is possible to conceive of a frequency distribution to represent the distribution of attitude in a specified group on the subject of pacifism-militarism.

Consider the ordinate of the frequency distribution at any point on the base line. The point and its immediate vicinity represent for our purpose an attitude, and we want to know relatively how common that degree of feeling for or against pacifism may be in the group that is being studied. It is of secondary interest to know that a particular statement of opinion is indorsed by a certain proportion of that group. It is only to the extent that the opinion is representative of an attitude that it is useful for our purposes. Later we shall consider the possibility that a statement of opinion may be scaled as rather pacifistic and yet be indorsed by a person of very pronounced militaristic sympathies. To the extent that the statement is indorsed or rejected by factors other than the attitude variable that it represents, to that extent the

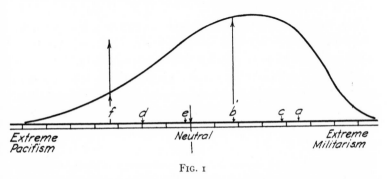

FIG. 1

statement is useless for our purposes. We shall also consider an objective criterion for spotting such statements so that they may be eliminated from the scale. In our entire study we shall be dealing, then, with opinions, not primarily because of their cognitive content but rather because they serve as the carriers or symbols of the attitudes of the people who express or indorse these opinions.

There is some ambiguity in using the term attitude in the plural. An attitude is represented as a point on the attitude continuum. Consequently there is an infinite number of attitudes that might be represented along the attitude scale. In practice, however, we do not differentiate so finely. In fact, an attitude, practically speaking, is represented by a certain narrow range or vicinity on the scale. When a frequency distribution is drawn for any continuous variable, such as stature, we classify the variable for descriptive purposes into steps, or class-intervals. The attitude variable can also be divided into class-intervals and the frequency counted in each class-interval. When we speak of "an" attitude, we shall refer to a point, or restricted range, on the attitude continuum. Several attitudes will be considered not as a set of discrete entities but as a series of class-intervals along the attitude scale.

A FREQUENCY DISTRIBUTION OF ATTITUDES

The main argument so far has been to show that since in ordinary conversation we readily and understandably describe individuals as more and less pacifistic or more and less militaristic in attitude, we may frankly represent this linearity in the form of a unidimensional scale. This has been done in a diagrammatic way in Figure 1. We shall first describe our objective and then show how a rational unit of measurement may be adopted for the whole scale.

Let the base line of Figure 1 represent a continuous range of attitudes from extreme pacifism on the left to extreme militarism on the right. If the various steps in such a scale were defined, it is clear that a person's attitude on militarism-pacifism could be represented by a point on that scale. The strength and direction of a particular individual's sympathies might be indicated by the point a, thus showing that he is rather militaristic in his opinions. Another individual might be represented at the point b to show that although he is slightly militaristic in his opinions, he is not so extreme about it as the person who is placed at the point a. A third person might be placed at the point c to show that he is quite militaristic and that the difference between a and c is very slight. A similar interpretation might be extended to any point on the continuous scale from extreme militarism to extreme pacifism, with a neutral or indifference zone between them.

A second characteristic might also be indicated graphically in terms of the scale, namely, the range of opinions that any particular individual is willing to indorse. It is of course not to be expected that every person will find only one single opinion on the whole scale that he is willing to indorse and that he will reject all the others. As a matter of fact we should probably find ourselves willing to indorse several opinions within a certain range of the scale. It is conceivable, then, that a pacifistically inclined person would be willing to indorse all or most of the opinions in the range *d* to *e* and that he would reject as too extremely pacifistic most of the opinions to the left of *d*, and would also reject the whole range of militaristic opinions. His attitude would then be indicated by the average or mean of the range that he indorses, unless he cares to select a particular opinion which most nearly represents his own attitude. The same sort of reasoning may of course be extended to the whole range of the scale, so that we should have at least two, or possibly three, characteristics of each person designated in terms of the scale. These characteristics would be (1) the mean position that he occupies on the scale; (2) the range of opinions that he is willing to accept, and (3) that one opinion which he selects as the one which most nearly represents his own attitude on the issue at stake.

It should also be possible to describe a *group* of individuals by means of the scale. This type of description has been represented in a diagrammatic way by the frequency outline.

Any ordinate of the curve represents the number of individuals, or the percentage of the whole group, that indorses the corresponding opinion. For example, the ordinate at *b* represents the number of persons in the group who indorse the degree of militarism indicated by the point *b* on the scale. A glance at the frequency curve shows that for the fictitious group of this diagram militaristic opinions are indorsed more frequently than the pacifistic ones. It is clear that the area of this frequency diagram represents the total number of indorsements given by the group. The diagram can be arranged in several different ways that will be separately discussed. It is sufficient at this moment to realize that, given a valid scale of opinions, it would be possible to compare several different groups in their attitudes on a disputed question.

A second type of group comparison might be made by the range or spread that the frequency surfaces reveal. If one of the groups is represented by a frequency diagram of considerable range or scatter, then that group would be more heterogeneous on the issue at stake than some other group whose frequency diagram of attitudes shows a smaller range or scatter. It goes without saying that the frequent assumption of a normal distribution in educational scale construction has absolutely no application here, because there is no reason whatever to assume that any group of people will be normally distributed in their opinions about anything.

It should be possible, then, to make four types of description by means of a scale of attitudes. These are (1) the average or mean attitude of a particular individual on the issue at stake; (2) the range of opinion that he is willing to accept or tolerate; (3) the relative popularity of each attitude of the scale for a designated group as shown by the frequency distribution for that group, and (4) the degree of homogeneity or heterogeneity in the attitudes of a designated group on the issue, as shown by the spread or dispersion of its frequency distribution.

This constitutes our objective. The heart of the problem is in the unit of measurement for the base line, and it is to this aspect of the problem that we may now turn.

A UNIT OF MEASUREMENT FOR ATTITUDES

The only way in which we can identify the different attitudes (points on the base line) is to use a set of opinions as landmarks, as it were, for the different parts or steps of the scale. The final scale will then consist of a series of statements of opinion, each of which is allocated to a particular point on the base line. If we start with enough statements, we may be able to select a list of forty or fifty opinions so chosen that they represent an evenly graduated series of attitudes. The separation between successive statements of opinion would then be uniform, but the scale can be constructed with a series of opinions allocated on the base line even though their base line separations are not uniform. For the purpose of drawing frequency distributions it will be convenient, however, to have the statements so chosen that the steps between them are uniform throughout the whole range of the scale.

Consider the three statements, a, c, and d, in Figure 1. The statements c and a are placed close together to indicate that they are very similar, while statements c and d are spaced far apart to indicate that they are very different. We should expect two individuals scaled at c and a, respectively, to agree very well in discussing pacifism and militarism. On the other hand, we should expect to be able to tell the difference quite readily between the opinions of a person at d and another person at c. The scale separations of the opinions must agree with our impressions of them.

In order to ascertain how far apart the statements should be on the final scale, one method, the method used in our experiment, is to submit them to a group of several hundred people who are asked to arrange the statements in order from the most pacifistic to the most militaristic. We do not ask them for their own opinions. That is another matter entirely. We are now concerned with the construction of a scale with a valid unit of measurement. There may be a hundred statements in the original list, and the several hundred persons are asked merely to arrange the statements in rank order according to the designated attitude variable. It is then possible to ascertain the proportion of the readers who consider statement a to be more militaristic than statement c. If the two statements represent very similar attitudes we should not expect to find perfect agreement in the rank order of statements a and c. If they are identical in attitude, there will be about 50 per cent of the readers who say that statement a is more militaristic than statement c, while the remaining 50 per cent of the readers will say that statement c is more militaristic than statement a. It is possible to use the proportion of readers or judges who agree about the rank order of any two statements as a basis for actual measurement.

If 90 per cent of the judges or readers say that statement a is more militaristic than statement b $(p_{a>b}=0.90)$ and if only 60 per cent of the readers say that statement a is more militaristic than statement c $(p_{a>c}=0.60)$ then clearly the scale separation $(a-c)$ is shorter than the scale separation $(a-b)$. The psychological scale separation between any two stimuli can be measured in terms of a law of comparative judgment.[1]

The practical outcome of this procedure is a series of statements of opinion allocated along the base line of Figure 1. The interpretation of the base-line distances is that the apparent difference between any two opinions will be equal to the apparent difference between any other two opinions which are spaced equally far apart on the scale. In other words, the shift in opinion represented by a unit distance on the base line seems to most people the same as the shift in opinion represented by a unit distance at any other part of the scale. Two individuals who are separated by any given distance on the scale *seem* to differ in their attitudes as much as any other two individuals with the same scale separation. In this sense we have a truly rational base line, and the frequency diagrams erected on such a base line are capable of legitimate interpretation as frequency surfaces.[2]

[1] For a more detailed discussion of this law see L. L. Thurstone, "The Law of Comparative Judgment," *Psychological Review*, July, 1927. The logic of the psychological S-scale is discussed in L. L. Thurstone, "Psychophysical Analysis," *American Journal of Psychology*, July, 1927.

[2] A detailed application of the law of comparative judgment to a related problem in attitude measurement is described in L. L. Thurstone, "An Experimental Study of Nationality Preferences," *Journal of General Psychology*, I (July-October, 1928).

In contrast with such a rational base line or scale is the simpler procedure of merely listing from ten to twenty opinions, arranging them in rank order by a few readers, and then merely counting the number of indorsements for each statement. That can of course be done provided that the resulting diagram is not interpreted as a frequency distribution of attitude. If so interpreted the diagram can be made to take any shape we please by merely adding new statements or eliminating some of them, arranging the resulting list in rank order evenly spaced on the base line. Allport's diagrams of opinions[1] are not frequency distributions. They should be considered as bar-diagrams in which is shown the frequency with which each of a number of statements is indorsed. Allport's pioneering studies in this field should be read by every investigator of this problem. Our own interest in the possibility of measuring attitude by means of opinions was started by Allport's article, and the present study is primarily a refinement of his statistical methods.

The ideal unit of measurement for the scale of attitudes is the standard deviation of the dispersion projected on the psychophysical scale of attitudes by a statement of opinion, chosen as a standard. It is a matter of indifference which statement is chosen as a standard, since the scales produced by using different statements as standards will have proportional scale-values. This mental unit of measurement is roughly comparable to, but not identical with, the so-called "just noticeable difference" in psychophysical measurement.[2] In the present experimental study another unit of measurement was used which will be subsequently described.

The reason why this ideal unit of measurement, the discrim-

[1] Floyd H. Allport, and D. A. Hartman, "Measurement and Motivation of Atypical Opinion in a Certain Group," *American Political Science Review*, XIX (1925), 735–60.

[2] L. L. Thurstone, "A Mental Unit of Measurement," *Journal of Educational Psychology*, May, 1927; "Equally Often Noticed Differences," *Psychological Review*, November, 1927.

inal error, could not be used in the present study is as follows: The law of comparative judgment can be used in two ways, neither of which was directly applicable to the present problem for practical rather than for logical reasons. One of these methods is to submit all of the stimuli, in pairs, to the subjects for judgment. Each one of the stimuli is submitted to every subject in combination with every other stimulus in the whole series. For example, two statements would be given to the subject with the request that he indicate which of them is more in favor of the church. When all of the subjects have made their judgments about this pair of statements we can ascertain the proportion, $p_{a > b}$, of the subjects who think that statement a is more strongly in favor of the church than statement b.

This can of course be done but the task becomes prohibitive, practically, in two ways. In the first place the subjects would be fatigued or bored if they had to make this type of judgment for

$$\frac{n\,(n-1)}{2} = \frac{130 \times 129}{2} = 8,385$$

pairs of statements, each pair requiring careful reading.

In the second place the statistical labor required to determine the scale-values would also be prohibitive although it is more conceivable than to ask several hundred individuals to read 8,385 pairs of statements.

When the stimuli are more easily and quickly judged than the comparison of two statements, the law of comparative judgment can be readily applied. For example, when the stimuli consist of pairs of nationalities in which the subject is asked only to underline the nationality that he would in general prefer to associate with, or when the stimuli consist of handwriting specimens presented in pairs so that the subject need only check that specimen which seems the more excellent, then the procedure is not so fatiguing.

The usual psychophysical problem does not involve so many

stimuli in each series and the number of judgments is thereby reduced to a more reasonable magnitude. The statistical labor is also reduced to proportions more easily handled when the stimulus series is not so long.

Another procedure for the law of comparative judgment is to ask the subject to sort all of the specimens in a series in rank order. When the psychophysical series is much shorter, from fifteen to twenty or even forty, then the task of arranging the stimuli in rank order is not so forbidding. But when the stimulus series consists of 130 statements, most of which must be read every time the subject looks at them for sorting into a rank order, the task becomes unwieldy. Furthermore, the statistical procedures required to extract the proportions, $p_{a>b}$, for every possible pair of stimuli from absolute rank order data is very laborious.

For these practical reasons it was advisable to use another psychophysical method in the construction of our attitude scale. We decided to use the method of equal-appearing intervals which has long been in use in psychophysical experimentation. The detailed experimental application of this method to the construction of our attitude scale will now be described.

CHAPTER II

CONSTRUCTION OF AN ATTITUDE SCALE

COLLECTION OF OPINIONS FOR THE SCALE

Several groups of people and many individuals were asked to write out their opinions about the church, and current literature was searched for suitable brief statements that might serve the purposes of the scale. By editing such material a list of 130 statements was prepared, expressive of attitudes covering as far as possible all gradations from one end of the scale to the other.

It was sometimes necessary to give special attention to the neutral statements. If a random compilation of statements of opinion should fail to produce neutral statements, there is some danger that the scale will break in two parts. The whole range of attitudes must be fairly well covered, as far as one can tell by preliminary inspection, in order to insure that there will be overlapping in the rank orders of different readers throughout the scale.

In making the initial list of statements several practical criteria were applied in the first editing work. Some of the important criteria are as follows: (1) The statements should be as brief as possible so as not to fatigue the subjects who are asked to read the whole list. (2) The statements should be such that they can be indorsed or rejected in accordance with their agreement or disagreement with the attitude of the reader. Some statements in a random sample will be so phrased that the reader can express no definite indorsement or rejection of them. (3) Every statement should be such that acceptance or rejection of the statement does indicate something regarding the reader's attitude about the issue in question. If, for example, the statement is made that war is an incentive to inventive genius, the acceptance or rejection of it really does not say anything regarding the reader's pacifistic or militaristic tendencies. He may regard the statement as an unquestioned fact and simply indorse it as a fact, in which case his answer has not revealed anything concerning his own attitude on the issue in question. However, only the conspicuous examples of this effect should be eliminated by inspection, because an objective criterion is available for detecting such statements so that their elimination from the scale will be automatic. Personal judgment should be minimized as far as possible in this type of work. (4) Double-barreled statements should be avoided except possibly as examples of neutrality when better neutral statements do not seem to be readily available. Double-barreled statements tend to have a high ambiguity. (5) One must insure that at least a fair majority of the statements really belong on the attitude variable that is to be measured. If a small number of irrelevant statements should be either intentionally or unintentionally left in the series, they will be automatically eliminated by an objective criterion, but the criterion will not be successful unless the majority of the statements are clearly a part of the stipulated variable.

The following is a list of the 130 statements about the church with which we began our experiments. The numbering is quite arbitrary and serves only for the purpose of identifying the statements in the various tables and diagrams.

LIST OF OPINIONS ABOUT THE CHURCH

1. I have seen no value in the church.
2. I believe the modern church has plenty of satisfying interests for young people.
3. I do not hear discussions in the church that are scientific or practical and so I do not care to go.
4. I believe that membership in a good church increases one's self-respect and usefulness.
5. I believe a few churches are trying to keep up to date in thinking and methods of work, but most are far behind the times.
6. I regard the church as an ethical society promoting the best way of living for both an individual and for society.

7. The paternal and benevolent attitude of the church is quite distasteful to me.

8. I believe the church has a good influence on the lower and uneducated classes but has no value for the upper, educated classes.

9. I don't believe church-going will do anyone any harm.

10. I have no interest in the church for my parents had no religion and I have seen no value in it.

11. I believe in the church and its teachings because I have been accustomed to them since I was a child.

12. I feel the churches are too narrow-minded and clannish.

13. I believe in religion but I seldom go to church.

14. I think the church allows denominational differences to appear larger than true religion.

15. I think the church is a good thing. I don't go much myself but I like my children to go.

16. I get no satisfaction from going to church.

17. In the church I find my best companions and express my best self.

18. I am an atheist and have no use for the church.

19. I feel church attendance is a fair index of the nation's morality.

20. I go to church because I enjoy music. I am in the choir and get musical training and chorus-singing.

21. I do not understand the dogmas or creeds of the church but I find that the church helps me to be more honest and creditable.

22. I believe in personal religion but organized religion as represented in the church has no meaning for me.

23. I am interested in a church that is beautiful and that emphasizes the aesthetic side of life.

24. The churches may be doing good and useful work but they do not interest me.

25. I believe the churches are doing far more harm than good.

26. I regard the church today as primarily an educational institution.

27. I believe in sincerity and goodness without any church ceremonies.

28. I believe in what the church teaches but with mental reservations.

29. My only interest in the church is in the opportunities it gives for a good time.

30. I believe the church ought to have a value but I regret that I have to quit it as it is.

31. I believe the church promotes a fine brotherly relationship between people and nations.

32. I believe the church is bound hand and foot by money interests and cannot practice the religion of Jesus.
33. I feel the church is petty, always quarreling over matters that have no interest or importance.
34. Sometimes I feel that the church and religion are necessary and sometimes I doubt it.
35. I go to church because my girl does.
36. I believe the churches are too much divided by factions and denominations to be a strong force for righteousness.
37. I am only interested in the church for the sake of the social life I find there.
38. I think too much money is being spent on the church for the benefit that is being derived.
39. I believe the church is absolutely needed to overcome the tendency to individualism and selfishness. It practices the golden rule fairly well.
40. I think the teaching of the church is altogether too superficial to have much social significance.
41. I think the country would be better off if the churches were closed and ministers set to some useful work.
42. I believe the church provides most of the leaders for every movement for social welfare.
43. I believe the church represents outgrown primitive beliefs that are based largely on fears.
44. I believe the church is the greatest institution in our country for developing patriotism.
45. Some churches are all right, but others are "all bunk."
46. I do not think the church is essential to Christianity.
47. I like our church for it gives young people a chance to have some fun and yet it is religious.
48. The church represents shallowness, hypocrisy, and prejudice.
49. I do not think one has to belong to the church to be religious.
50. I feel the church services give me inspiration and help me to live up to my best during the following week.
51. I feel I can worship God better out of doors than in the church and I get more inspiration there.
52. I believe interest in the church is more emotional than rational.
53. I feel that the church is rapidly coming to apply scientific methods to its thinking and its promotion of religion.
54. When I go to church I enjoy a fine ritual service with good music.

55. I believe that if young people are not interested in the church it is the fault of either their parents or the church leaders.
56. I believe the church is losing ground as education advances.
57. The church has not helped me to any satisfactory ideas of God or the future. I have had to work out my own ideas.
58. I think one church is about as good as another but some camouflage better than others.
59. I go to church occasionally but have no specific attitude toward it.
60. I believe orthodox religion is all right but radicals upset the influence of the church.
61. I go to church because I find the sermon usually interesting.
62. I am interested in the church because of its work for moral and social reform in which I desire to share.
63. I believe the church would be all right if it kept close to the teachings of Jesus but it does not and so fails.
64. I feel the need for religion but do not find what I want in any one church.
65. I think the church is a parasite on society.
66. I think the church is a place for religious instruction of young and old and is essential in every community.
67. I think the church is after money all the time and I am tired of hearing of it.
68. I think the church and organized religion is necessary for the superstitious and uneducated but it should become less and less important.
69. I am careless about religion and church relationships but I would not like to see my attitude become general.
70. I like the opportunity in the young people's society for discussion and self-expression.
71. I think the church is valuable for creating ideals and for setting a person right morally.
72. I think the organized church is an enemy of science and truth.
73. I like to go to church for I get something worth while to think about and it keeps my mind filled with right thoughts.
74. I enjoy my church because there is a spirit of friendliness there.
75. I believe the church is the greatest influence for good government and right living.
76. The church is to me primarily a place to commune with God.
77. I do not receive any benefit from attending church services but I think it helps some people.

78. I give my money to support the church but I keep out of it because there is so much petty jangling.
79. I believe the church leaders are afraid to stand up and say what is true and right. The church is weak.
80. I enjoy a good church service but do not take much stock in the teachings.
81. If I were picking a man for a responsible job I would give the preference to a regular church-member.
82. The church does not interest me now but sometime I expect I shall find it worth while to join.
83. I am attracted to the church by its courageous attack on what is commonly called impossible.
84. I find the social life of the church too slow and uninteresting and that is all I care about.
85. I believe the church has done and can do far more for society than any organization of science.
86. My belief is that the church is more spiritual and a greater force for good than it was a hundred years ago. It is increasing in value.
87. I think the church is hundreds of years behind the times and cannot make a dent of modern life.
88. I like church occasionally but do not feel that one should get too ardent about worship or church-going.
89. I believe the church has grown up with the primary purpose of perpetuating the spirit and teachings of Jesus and deserves loyal support.
90. I like the ceremonies of my church but do not miss them much when I stay away.
91. I regard the church as the institution for the development of spiritual life individually and socially.
92. I believe the church is far removed from the essentials of Christian love and brotherly kindness.
93. I believe church-membership is almost essential to living life at its best.
94. I believe the church is as necessary as the school for our social life.
95. I do not believe in any brand of religion or in any particular church but I have never given the subject serious thought.
96. I regard the church as a static, crystallized institution, and as such it is unwholesome and detrimental to society and the individual.
97. I think the church is learning more and more how to correlate science and religion for the good of humanity.

98. No one attempts to live up to the ideals of the church but it serves as a good stimulator.

99. To me the church is more or less boring.

100. I believe the church is a powerful agency for promoting both individual and social righteousness.

101. I believe the church is the greatest institution in America today.

102. I have no desire to attend, join, or have anything to do with any church I know.

103. I find the services of the church both restful and inspiring.

104. I find more satisfaction in doing church work than in anything else I do.

105. I think the church is more controlled by magic than by reason.

106. I believe the average of the morals of church-members is considerably higher than the average of non-church-members in the same social status.

107. The church is needed to develop religion which has always been concerned with man's deepest feelings and greatest values.

108. I believe the church is full of hypocrites and have no use for it.

109. I never want to miss church for I always get an inspiration from a good church service.

110. I think the church keeps business and politics up to a higher standard than they would otherwise tend to maintain.

111. I think the average church has a deadening influence and prevents true religion.

112. I believe in the ideals of the church but I am tired of denominationalism.

113. I feel the church perpetuates the values which man puts highest in his philosophy of life.

114. I believe the church is fundamentally sound but some of its adherents have given it a bad name.

115. I cannot think through the mysteries of religion but like to get the assurances of reality, of God, and immortality that the church gives and stands for.

116. I believe the majority of church-members are shameless hypocrites. They do not practice what they pretend to do and do not care.

117. I believe the church is working steadily for the application of the principles of Jesus to all personal-social relationships.

118. I believe the church is an excellent character-building institution for children.

119. I think the church is a hindrance to true religion for it still depends upon magic, superstition, and myth.

120. I think the church is a divine institution and deserves the highest respect and loyalty.
121. I believe churches are as essential to religion as schools are to education.
122. I think the church is cursed by a narrow-minded, selfish lot of people.
123. I think the church is necessary but it puts its emphasis on the wrong things.
124. I support the church because I think it is the most unselfish and idealistic institution in society.
125. I respect any church-member's beliefs but I think it is all "bunk."
126. I believe the church develops friendships and ideals that help one to reject low and evil purposes and acts.
127. I think the church seeks to impose a lot of worn-out dogmas and medieval superstitions.
128. My experience is that the church is hopelessly out of date.
129. I believe the church is doing a good work but will have to work on a seven-day-a-week program if it is going to keep up with the job.
130. I believe the church is a changing human institution but it has divine realities behind it. The spirit of God moves through it.

It will of course be noticed that some of these statements are ambiguous and that others are unsuitable for the present scale because their acceptance or rejection does not indicate whether the indorser is really in favor of the church or against it. In fact, many of the statements in this list violate the several criteria that we have mentioned, but there was a definite plan in leaving these defective statements in the list. Since there was available a criterion of ambiguity and a criterion of irrelevance, it was thought best to retain defective statements in the experimental list so as to see whether these undesirable statements would be eliminated by the objective criteria. It is undoubtedly desirable so to devise the technique of attitude scale construction that a minimum is left for the personal judgment of the investigator as regards the value of statements of opinion for the scale. It will later be seen that on the whole the most defective statements are fairly well eliminated by the objective criteria.

THE SORTING PROCEDURE

In the present study the subjects were asked to sort the 130 statements into eleven piles to represent an evenly graduated series of attitudes from those extremely against the church to those which are very much in favor of the church. *It should be noted that in sorting the statements the subject did not express his own opinions about the church.* He was not asked to state what he believed about any religious issue. He was asked merely to sort the statements into the eleven piles, and we think that this sorting will be done similarly by those who favor the church and by those who are antagonistic to the church.

The 130 statements were mimeographed on small slips, one statement on each slip. A set of these 130 slips was given to each subject. He was also given eleven master-slips of the same size lettered from *A* to *K*. Only three of these slips were labeled as to the kind of opinions that should be placed on them, namely *A*, which contained the statement, "This pile expresses highest appreciation of the church"; *K*, which contained the statement, "This pile expresses strongest depreciation of the church," and the slip *F*, which contained the statement, "This pile contains only neutral expressions."

It is a fundamentally important matter that the eleven piles should not be described except to give a starting-point such as neutrality and the two ends. If the eleven piles were defined by descriptive phrases such as is customary on rating scales of various kinds, the fundamental characteristic of the present measurement method would be destroyed. The reason for this is that the intervals between successive piles should be apparently equal shifts of opinion as judged by the subject. If they were labeled by descriptive phrases such as the steps in a graphic rating scale, the intervals would be defined by the descriptive phrases and there would be no guaranty that the successive intervals appear equal to the subjects. The intervals, if described by the investigator, would be arbitrary and set by him. It is essential that the subject

be given the freedom to adjust the slips in the piles so that the
intervals in attitude from one pile to the next seem to him to be
equal. That is the unit of measurement for the present scale.

The detailed instructions given to the subject were as follows:

DIRECTIONS FOR SORTING SLIPS

1. The 130 slips contain statements regarding the value of the church.
   These have been made by various persons, students, and others.
2. As a first step in the making of a scale that may be used in a test of opinions relating to the church and religion we want a number of persons to
   sort these 130 slips into eleven piles.
3. You are given eleven slips with letters on them, *A, B, C, D, E, F, G, H,
   I, J, K*. Please arrange these before you in regular order. On slip *A* put
   those statements which you believe express the highest *appreciation* of
   the value of the church. On slip *F* put those expressing a neutral position. On slip *K* put those slips which express the strongest *depreciation* of
   the church. On the rest of the slips arrange statements in accordance
   with the degree of appreciation or depreciation expressed in them.
4. This means that when you are through sorting you will have eleven piles
   arranged in order of value-estimate from *A*, the highest, to *K*, the lowest.
5. Do not try to get the same number in each pile. They are not evenly
   distributed.
6. The numbers on the slips are code numbers and have nothing to do with
   the arrangement in piles.
7. You will find it easier to sort them if you look over a number of the slips,
   chosen at random, before you begin to sort.
8. It will probably take you about forty-five minutes to sort them.
9. When you are through sorting, please clip the piles together, each with
   its letter slip on top. Replace the eleven sets, clipped carefully, in the
   big envelope and return to E. J. Chave, Room 306, Swift Hall, University
   of Chicago.
10. Put your name and university classification on slip inclosed.

Each subject was asked to indicate by number the two statements in each of the eleven piles which seemed to him to be most
representative of that pile. This was intended to facilitate the
selection of the statements to be used in the final scale but it is
doubtful whether this procedure will be retained in this form in
future scale construction.

The returns were tabulated so as to show for each subject the pile in which he placed every one of the 130 statements. From such a tabulation the data were assembled into Table I, which is a summary of the sorting of the 130 statements by 300 subjects. The first column of the table gives the code number of the statements by which they may be easily identified. The next two columns contain the scale-value and the Q-value, which is a measure of the ambiguity of each statement. These two measurements will be explained in a later paragraph. The remaining columns give the accumulative frequencies for each statement. The interpretation of this part of the table for statement No. 1 as an example is as follows. None of the 300 subjects placed statement No. 1 in any of the first five piles. This is indicated by the entries of 0.00 in each of the first five columns. In this group 8 per cent placed this statement in pile F; 17 per cent placed it in F or G; 23 per cent placed it in F, G, or H; 33 per cent placed it in pile I or to the left of that pile; 52 per cent placed it in pile J or to the left of that pile, while all of them placed this statement in pile K or somewhere to the left of K.

THE CONSISTENCY OF THE INDIVIDUAL SUBJECT

In an experiment of this sort in which large numbers of subjects participate, and in which the experimenter does not have the opportunity to observe each subject at work, one must expect that some subjects will do their task in a perfunctory or careless manner. It is also possible that some subjects fail to understand the experiment or fail to read the mimeographed instructions carefully enough to understand just what is wanted. It has seemed desirable, therefore, to set up some criterion by which we could identify those individual records which were so inconsistent that they should be eliminated from our tabulations. The labor of tabulating the data is considerable, and we are justified in eliminating those individual subjects who have not responded with sufficient care or interest.

SUMMARY OF SORTING OF 130 STATEMENTS BY 300 PERSONS

TABLE I

STATE-MENT	SCALE-VALUE	Q	A	B	C	D	E	F	G	H	I	J	K
			0–1	1–2	2–3	3–4	4–5	5–6	6–7	7–8	8–9	9–10	10–11
1....	9.9	2.4	.00	.00	.00	.00	.00	.08	.17	.23	.33	.52	1.00
2....	3.4	1.3	.02	.13	.35	.72	.93	.97	.98	.99	1.00	1.00	1.00
3....	7.6	1.9	.00	.00	.01	.01	.01	.09	.33	.60	.84	.98	1.00
4....	2.7	1.5	.06	.26	.60	.91	.98	.99	1.00	1.00	1.00	1.00	1.00
5....	6.4	2.4	.01	.02	.03	.11	.29	.39	.64	.86	.96	.99	1.00
6....	2.0	1.7	.21	.51	.76	.86	.96	.98	.99	.99	.99	1.00	1.00
7....	8.2	2.0	.00	.00	.00	.01	.01	.03	.20	.45	.71	.94	1.00
8....	6.7	3.6	.00	.01	.02	.09	.27	.41	.54	.67	.81	.93	1.00
9....	5.3	0.7	.01	.02	.03	.06	.25	.87	.93	.96	.98	1.00	1.00
10....	8.6	3.0	.00	.00	.00	.00	.00	.14	.27	.41	.58	.79	1.00
11....	4.0	1.2	.01	.04	.18	.47	.84	.94	.97	.98	.99	.99	1.00
12....	8.4	1.9	.00	.00	.01	.02	.05	.07	.18	.42	.71	.92	1.00
13....	5.4	1.5	.01	.01	.02	.09	.34	.69	.84	.91	.97	.99	1.00
14....	7.2	1.9	.01	.02	.03	.04	.12	.15	.44	.72	.90	.99	1.00
15....	4.4	1.2	.00	.03	.13	.38	.80	.90	.94	.97	.99	.99	1.00
16....	8.2	2.7	.00	.00	.00	.00	.01	.10	.30	.47	.66	.84	1.00
17....	2.0	1.7	.21	.49	.77	.92	.97	.99	.99	.99	1.00	1.00	1.00
18....	10.8	1.8	.00	.00	.00	.00	.00	.03	.06	.09	.13	.28	1.00
19....	2.6	1.5	.08	.30	.66	.87	.95	.98	.99	1.00	1.00	1.00	1.00
20....	4.5	1.3	.00	.01	.06	.28	.71	.82	.89	.96	.98	.99	1.00
21....	3.1	1.4	.02	.13	.48	.80	.92	.95	.97	.98	.99	.99	1.00
22....	7.1	2.3	.00	.00	.00	.03	.07	.23	.49	.67	.84	.93	1.00
23....	4.1	1.5	.01	.05	.18	.47	.81	.90	.94	.97	.99	1.00	1.00
24....	5.9	1.7	.00	.00	.00	.01	.05	.56	.74	.81	.89	.95	1.00
25....	10.5	1.6	.00	.00	.00	.00	.01	.01	.02	.04	.12	.35	1.00
26....	3.6	2.2	.02	.11	.35	.59	.79	.88	.95	.97	.99	1.00	1.00
27....	6.7	1.9	.00	.01	.02	.05	.09	.28	.60	.78	.90	.96	1.00
28....	4.5	2.0	.01	.02	.10	.31	.65	.77	.86	.95	.98	.99	1.00
29....	5.1	2.7	.00	.00	.01	.08	.48	.61	.73	.82	.89	.96	1.00
30....	7.1	2.2	.00	.00	.00	.01	.08	.17	.47	.68	.82	.94	1.00
31....	1.7	1.3	.23	.62	.88	.96	.98	.99	.99	1.00	1.00	1.00	1.00
32....	9.4	1.9	.00	.01	.01	.03	.04	.05	.08	.19	.38	.69	1.00
33....	8.6	1.7	.00	.00	.00	.01	.02	.03	.13	.32	.65	.88	1.00
34....	5.6	0.8	.00	.01	.01	.01	.11	.84	.89	.94	.98	.99	1.00
35....	5.6	1.7	.00	.00	.01	.03	.21	.67	.76	.83	.89	.95	1.00
36....	7.2	1.9	.01	.01	.04	.06	.13	.19	.44	.70	.88	.99	1.00
37....	5.2	2.4	.00	.00	.01	.11	.51	.64	.75	.86	.94	.97	1.00
38....	7.5	1.9	.00	.00	.01	.03	.07	.11	.36	.63	.85	.98	1.00
39....	1.8	1.3	.16	.57	.85	.95	.99	.99	.99	1.00	1.00	1.00	1.00
40....	8.3	2.0	.00	.00	.00	.01	.05	.08	.21	.43	.71	.93	1.00
41....	10.5	1.0	.00	.00	.00	.00	.00	.01	.02	.03	.09	.24	1.00
42....	2.0	1.4	.12	.52	.81	.94	.98	.99	.99	.99	.99	1.00	1.00
43....	9.2	1.6	.00	.00	.00	.01	.02	.04	.07	.19	.43	.79	1.00
44....	2.6	2.0	.08	.33	.61	.79	.91	.92	.94	.96	.97	.98	1.00
45....	6.0	2.5	.00	.01	.02	.03	.12	.50	.65	.75	.86	.96	1.00
46....	7.5	3.0	.00	.00	.02	.03	.06	.20	.42	.56	.73	.86	1.00
47....	3.8	1.5	.01	.06	.26	.58	.91	.96	.97	.99	.99	1.00	1.00
48....	10.4	1.4	.00	.00	.00	.00	.01	.01	.02	.04	.10	.34	1.00
49....	6.3	1.6	.01	.02	.05	.06	.09	.40	.72	.85	.94	.98	1.00
50....	1.7	1.4	.23	.60	.86	.98	.99	.99	.99	1.00	1.00	1.00	1.00
51....	6.9	1.7	.00	.01	.01	.03	.08	.21	.54	.76	.91	.98	1.00
52....	6.8	1.9	.00	.01	.03	.05	.17	.28	.56	.79	.90	.98	1.00
53....	2.8	1.8	.06	.26	.57	.78	.91	.96	.98	.99	.99	.99	1.00
54....	4.0	1.4	.00	.05	.21	.48	.85	.93	.96	.98	.99	1.00	1.00
55....	4.2	2.4	.00	.07	.26	.47	.67	.85	.93	.97	.99	1.00	1.00
56....	7.4	2.1	.00	.00	.01	.03	.08	.13	.41	.64	.80	.95	1.00
57....	7.8	2.3	.00	.00	.02	.02	.04	.11	.33	.54	.77	.91	1.00
58....	7.0	2.8	.00	.00	.00	.02	.10	.32	.51	.66	.83	.95	1.00
59....	5.5	0.7	.00	.00	.00	.02	.11	.81	.89	.91	.94	.97	1.00
60....	5.1	2.6	.00	.03	.07	.21	.48	.64	.75	.87	.94	.98	1.00
61....	3.9	1.4	.00	.04	.19	.56	.86	.94	.97	.98	.98	.99	1.00
62....	2.3	1.3	.11	.40	.78	.93	.97	.99	.99	.99	1.00	1.00	1.00
63....	7.6	2.4	.01	.01	.03	.06	.11	.16	.37	.58	.79	.93	1.00
64....	6.1	2.3	.00	.01	.05	.12	.29	.47	.72	.88	.93	.98	1.00
65....	11.00	1.4	.00	.00	.00	.00	.00	.01	.01	.03	.08	.18	1.00

TABLE I—*Continued*

STATE-MENT	SCALE-VALUE	Q	A	B	C	D	E	F	G	H	I	J	K
			0–1	1–2	2–3	3–4	4–5	5–6	6–7	7–8	8–9	9–10	10–1
66....	1.5	1.4	.34	.70	.93	.99	1.00	1.00	1.00	1.00	1.00	1.00	1.00
67....	9.0	1.6	.00	.00	.00	.00	.00	.01	.06	.22	.48	.80	1.00
68....	7.9	3.0	.00	.00	.00	.04	.21	.24	.38	.50	.73	.89	1.00
69....	4.7	1.4	.00	.01	.09	.20	.64	.82	.92	.95	.98	.99	1.00
70....	3.6	1.5	.02	.09	.30	.63	.92	.98	.99	1.00	1.00	1.00	1.00
71....	1.8	1.3	.16	.59	.85	.97	.99	1.00	1.00	1.00	1.00	1.00	1.00
72....	10.7	1.7	.00	.00	.00	.00	.01	.02	.02	.05	.10	.29	1.00
73....	2.2	1.5	.10	.42	.74	.95	.99	.99	.99	.99	.99	1.00	1.00
74....	3.3	1.4	.03	.13	.40	.77	.94	.98	1.00	1.00	1.00	1.00	1.00
75....	0.4	2.2	.63	.85	.95	.99	.99	1.00	1.00	1.00	1.00	1.00	1.00
76....	1.3	2.2	.41	.68	.84	.92	.97	.99	.99	1.00	1.00	1.00	1.00
77....	5.7	2.2	.00	.00	.01	.03	.33	.58	.74	.88	.95	.98	1.00
78....	6.4	2.5	.00	.00	.00	.05	.25	.39	.64	.77	.91	.98	1.00
79....	8.3	1.9	.01	.01	.02	.03	.06	.07	.20	.42	.69	.89	1.00
80....	5.4	2.2	.00	.00	.01	.10	.41	.64	.79	.89	.94	.98	1.00
81....	2.8	1.7	.06	.24	.57	.82	.96	.99	.99	.99	1.00	1.00	1.00
82....	5.3	1.5	.00	.00	.02	.04	.34	.71	.83	.90	.94	.97	1.00
83....	2.6	1.9	.10	.32	.61	.83	.93	.98	.98	.99	.99	.99	1.00
84....	7.8	2.1	.00	.00	.00	.01	.03	.03	.31	.55	.77	.92	1.00
85....	1.5	1.6	.31	.67	.82	.93	.97	.98	.99	.99	1.00	1.00	1.00
86....	1.8	1.7	.24	.58	.81	.92	.97	.99	.99	.99	1.00	1.00	1.00
87....	9.5	1.6	.00	.00	.00	.00	.01	.02	.05	.15	.34	.71	1.00
88....	5.4	2.4	.00	.00	.01	.05	.40	.61	.77	.88	.95	.99	1.00
89....	1.0	1.4	.50	.83	.95	.98	.99	1.00	1.00	1.00	1.00	1.00	1.00
90....	5.1	1.3	.00	.00	.02	.10	.46	.80	.91	.96	.99	1.00	1.00
91....	1.5	1.7	.37	.67	.90	.97	.99	1.00	1.00	1.00	1.00	1.00	1.00
92....	9.0	1.8	.00	.00	.01	.02	.03	.04	.09	.25	.49	.77	1.00
93....	1.5	1.2	.26	.70	.91	.97	.98	.99	.99	.99	.99	1.00	1.00
94....	2.0	1.5	.17	.52	.80	.93	.98	.99	.99	1.00	1.00	1.00	1.00
95....	5.9	2.6	.00	.00	.01	.01	.03	.51	.67	.75	.86	.95	1.00
96....	10.5	1.9	.00	.00	.00	.00	.01	.01	.01	.04	.13	.35	1.00
97....	2.5	1.9	.08	.35	.63	.87	.96	.98	1.00	1.00	1.00	1.00	1.00
98....	4.6	1.9	.00	.03	.10	.27	.66	.73	.86	.92	.96	.98	1.00
99....	7.6	2.2	.00	.00	.00	.01	.03	.09	.36	.58	.78	.94	1.00
100....	1.2	1.0	.40	.85	.95	.98	1.00	1.00	1.00	1.00	1.00	1.00	1.00
101....	0.2	1.4	.78	.91	.96	.97	.98	.99	.99	1.00	1.00	1.00	1.00
102....	9.6	2.3	.00	.00	.00	.00	.00	.11	.17	.24	.39	.60	1.00
103....	2.3	1.6	.14	.43	.74	.92	.98	.99	.99	1.00	1.00	1.00	1.00
104....	2.1	1.8	.18	.46	.72	.90	.96	.97	.99	.99	.99	.99	1.00
105....	9.0	1.6	.00	.00	.00	.01	.01	.03	.09	.23	.51	.84	1.00
106....	2.7	1.6	.03	.27	.61	.89	.98	.99	.99	1.00	1.00	1.00	1.00
107....	1.4	1.4	.36	.75	.90	.97	.98	.99	1.00	1.00	1.00	1.00	1.00
108....	10.5	1.6	.00	.00	.00	.00	.00	.01	.01	.03	.10	.32	1.00
109....	2.1	1.5	.15	.48	.77	.93	.98	.98	.99	.99	.99	.99	1.00
110....	2.6	1.6	.06	.31	.66	.88	.96	.97	.98	.99	1.00	1.00	1.00
111....	9.6	1.5	.00	.00	.01	.01	.01	.02	.04	.09	.30	.63	1.00
112....	4.6	2.2	.01	.05	.13	.35	.63	.74	.86	.94	.99	1.00	1.00
113....	0.8	1.6	.56	.84	.95	.98	.99	.99	1.00	1.00	1.00	1.00	1.00
114....	3.9	1.8	.02	.07	.25	.53	.80	.89	.93	.96	.99	1.00	1.00
115....	2.5	1.8	.12	.34	.66	.84	.94	.97	.98	.99	.99	1.00	1.00
116....	9.9	1.5	.00	.00	.00	.01	.02	.02	.03	.06	.18	.52	1.00
117....	1.1	1.7	.46	.75	.90	.97	.99	1.00	1.00	1.00	1.00	1.00	1.00
118....	2.3	1.7	.10	.40	.69	.88	.97	.98	.99	1.00	1.00	1.00	1.00
119....	9.6	1.3	.00	.00	.00	.00	.00	.01	.03	.08	.28	.66	1.00
120....	0.5	2.0	.65	.83	.92	.96	.98	1.00	1.00	1.00	1.00	1.00	1.00
121....	1.4	1.5	.31	.71	.88	.95	.99	1.00	1.00	1.00	1.00	1.00	1.00
122....	9.1	2.2	.00	.00	.01	.02	.05	.07	.12	.28	.49	.76	1.00
123....	5.3	2.4	.00	.01	.03	.15	.51	.61	.79	.92	.97	1.00	1.00
124....	1.1	2.0	.48	.72	.89	.97	.98	.99	.99	.99	.99	1.00	1.00
125....	8.8	2.1	.00	.00	.00	.01	.01	.07	.19	.32	.55	.83	1.00
126....	2.0	1.3	.12	.52	.84	.97	.99	1.00	1.00	1.00	1.00	1.00	1.00
127....	9.2	1.6	.00	.01	.01	.02	.02	.02	.05	.18	.44	.79	1.00
128....	9.1	1.8	.00	.00	.00	.00	.01	.02	.10	.21	.46	.76	1.00
129....	3.4	1.9	.04	.16	.39	.67	.88	.93	.98	.99	1.00	1.00	1.00
130....	1.4	1.8	.38	.68	.87	.92	.97	.98	.99	1.00	1.00	1.00	1.00

It is also an important consideration to avoid any criterion of inconsistency for the elimination of careless or indifferent subjects which may constitute in effect an artificial loading of the main results of the investigation. As a criterion for eliminating individual subjects we adopted the rule that any subject who placed 30 or more of the 130 statements in one of the eleven piles was excluded. This objective criterion eliminated a number of subjects who were known to do the sorting of the statements carelessly and still others who showed in conversation that they had evidently failed to understand the instructions. We do not believe that this is in any sense an infallible criterion but it has undoubtedly served to eliminate many of the subjects whose sortings were careless or who misunderstood the instructions. In the entire group of 341 subjects who participated in the original sorting of the 130 statements 41 were eliminated from our final tabulations by this criterion.

CHAPTER III
THE SCALE-VALUES
GRAPHICAL DETERMINATION OF THE SCALE-VALUES

The scale-values were determined graphically. In order to illustrate this procedure seven of the graphs are here reproduced, and they show several different types of statement of opinion. In Figure 2 statement No. 39 is represented. This graph is plotted directly from the accumulative proportions of Table I. The graph shows immediately that practically all of the subjects classified this statement in the five class-intervals most favorable to the church. The statement reads as follows: "I believe the church is absolutely needed to overcome the tendency to individualism and selfishness. It practices the golden rule fairly well." The curve of Figure 2 crosses the 50 per cent level at the interpolated scale-value of 1.8 which is assigned as the scale-value for this statement. The scale-value is such that half of the readers classified this statement as more favorable to the church than the position 1.8, while half of them placed the statement as less favorable to the church than this position in the series of eleven piles.

The scale-value is indicated by a small vertical arrowhead. On either side of the arrowhead is a small vertical line. These two vertical lines indicate the two quartile points for the curve. In Figure 2 the two vertical marks are located at scale-values of 1.3 and 2.6, respectively. The separation between these two marks is a measure of the ambiguity of the statement. In the present case the ambiguity, the Q-value, is 1.3, which is simply the difference between 2.6 and 1.3. If a statement is very ambiguous, the different readers will place it over a wide range on the scale and the Q-value will be correspondingly high. If the statement is interpreted with regard to the specified attitude variable rather consistently, if the statement is concise and uniform in the meaning which it conveys to all the readers, then they will place it at approximately the same position on the scale, and the Q-value will then be correspondingly small.

In Figure 3 a similar graph is drawn for statement No. 51, which reads: "I feel I can worship God better out of doors than in

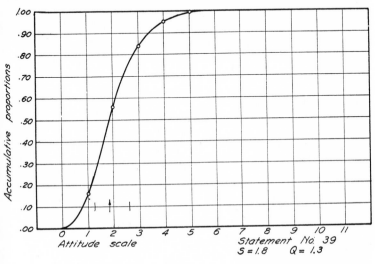

FIG. 2

the church and I get more inspiration there." This statement is clearly toward the other end of the scale and its scale-value is 6.9. The ambiguity, or Q-value, is 1.7.

Figure 4 has been included to show the psychometric graph for statement No. 9, which is judged rather uniformly. It has a low ambiguity. Its Q-value is only 0.7 with a scale value of 5.3. It is a neutral statement which is judged to be neutral by the great majority of the readers. The statement is, "I don't believe church-going will do anyone any harm." In contrast with this statement is No. 8 which is a very ambiguous one. It reads: "I believe the church has a good influence on the lower and uneducated classes

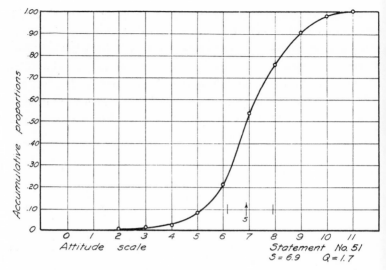

Fig. 3

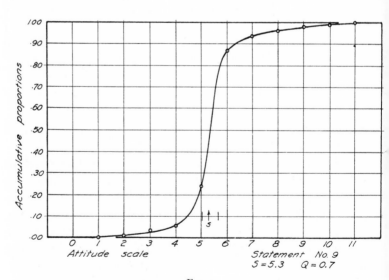

Fig. 4

but has no value for the upper, educated classes." This statement is represented in Figure 5, according to which the scale value is 6.7 and the ambiguity or Q-value is 3.6. Note that the statement spreads in a more or less rectangular distribution over eight class-intervals. This is a double-barreled statement, and it has been found that such statements turn out more frequently than not to be ambiguous. Such a statement is eliminated from the final scale

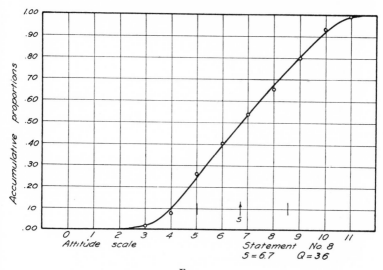

FIG. 5

on account of the objective measure of ambiguity which is given directly in the Q-value.

Figure 6 represents statement No. 28 and is included to show the appearance of the psychometric graph when it is continuous but skewed.

In Figure 7 we have a psychometric graph for statement No. 113 which more than half of the readers placed in the first of the eleven piles. Its scale-value can be obtained by extrapolation as shown in the graph whereby the scale-value is located slightly below the value of 1.00. In order to estimate the Q-value, the upper

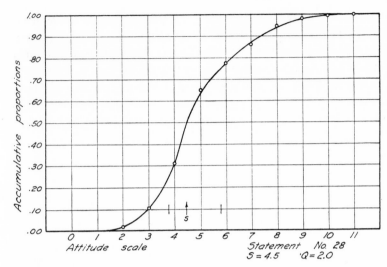

Fig. 6

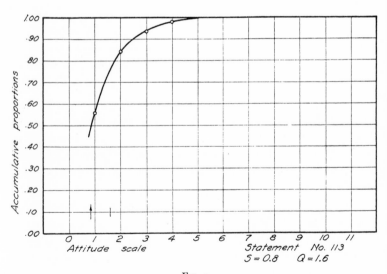

Fig. 7

quartile distance is doubled since the lower quartile is indeterminate. The lower quartile point might be determined by additional extrapolation but that is probably less desirable than to double the upper quartile distance as an estimated Q-value.

In Figure 8 we have the graph for statement No. 48. It is clearly judged to be at the anti-end of the scale. Its scale value can be determined by extrapolation. The curve is continued until

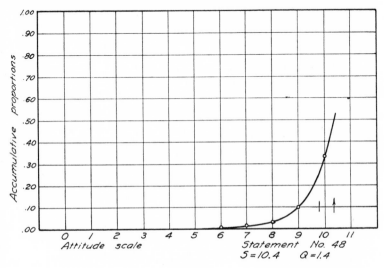

FIG. 8

it crosses the 50 per cent level, which is at approximately 10.4, and this is assigned as the scale-value of the statement. The Q-value is ascertained by doubling the difference between the median point and the lower quartile point. It should be noted that the entry of 1.00 in column K for statement 48 in Table I is ignored in drawing the curve of Figure 8. The entry in column K is always unity, and the ordinate at the point 11 is necessarily unity because all judgments which would place a statement beyond the point 11 are concentrated at the point 11. It does not represent the true ordinate at that point.

RELIABILITY OF THE SCALE-VALUES

An approximate estimate of the reliability of the scale-values may be obtained in the following manner: The Q-value is twice the quartile deviation of the distribution of each opinion on the subjective scale.
Hence

$$Q = 2q .$$

The average Q-value of the forty-five opinions in the experimental scale is 1.67 and consequently

$$q = \frac{Q}{2} = 0.84 .$$

The standard deviation of the distribution of scale-values is therefore, on the average,

$$\sigma_{dist} = \frac{q}{0.67} = 1.25 \text{ scale units} .$$

The scale-value of an opinion is the median of its distribution on the subjective scale. Hence, the standard error of the scale value is

$$\sigma_{med} = 1.25 \frac{\sigma}{\sqrt{n}}$$

$$= 0.09 \text{ when } n = 300 .$$

The probable error of the scale value is consequently

$$p.e._{md} = 0.67 \times 0.09 = 0.06 \text{ scale-units} .$$

This is a very satisfactory reliability for the scale-values which are recorded to one decimal in our tables.

In order further to test the stability of the scale-values in a practical way we ascertained the changes in scale-values brought about by increasing the number of subjects from 150 to 300. In order to make such a test, we tabulated the results for the first 150 subjects who sorted the 130 statements into eleven piles, subjectively equally spaced. The sorting was continued until 300 subjects had done it. The scale-values were then determined for the entire group of 300. The discrepancies between the first set of

TABLE II

FREQUENCY TABLE OF DIFFERENCES $d = |S_1 - S_2|$ BETWEEN THE SCALE-VALUES S_1 WHICH WERE DETERMINED FROM 150 SUBJECTS AND THE SCALE-VALUES S_2 WHICH WERE DETERMINED FROM THE ENTIRE GROUP OF 300 SUBJECTS

d	f	
-0.4	0	
-0.3	2	
-0.2	6	
-0.1	25	
0.0	64	Mean discrepancy for the whole
$+0.1$	19	list of 130 statements $= .074$
$+0.2$	10	
$+0.3$	2	
$+0.4$	2	
	—	
	130	

TABLE III

FREQUENCY TABLE OF DIFFERENCES $d = |S_1 - S_2|$ BETWEEN THE SCALE-VALUES S_1 WHICH WERE DETERMINED FROM 150 SUBJECTS AND THE SCALE-VALUES S_2 WHICH WERE DETERMINED FROM 300 SUBJECTS

d	f	
-0.4	0	
-0.3	0	
-0.2	2	
-0.1	4	Mean discrepancy for the 45 state-
0.0	29	ments in the experimental scale
$+0.1$	5	$= 0.056$
$+0.2$	4	
$+0.3$	0	
$+0.4$	1	
	—	
	45	

scale-values, determined by 150 subjects, and the final set of scale-values, determined by the entire group of 300 subjects, are summarized in Table II. The same kind of summary is shown in Table III for the discrepancies in the scale-values of the 45 statements chosen for the experimental scale. It is seen that the mean discrepancy between the scale-values from the data for 150 subjects and the scale-values from the 300 subjects is 0.074 scale-units for the entire set of 130 statements and 0.038 for the 45 statements in the experimental scale. These discrepancies are very small and they indicate that 300 subjects are quite sufficient to stabilize the scale-values for the method of equal-appearing intervals that we have used.

AN OBJECTIVE CRITERION OF AMBIGUITY

Inspection of the curves in Figures 2 to 8 inclusive reveals that some of the statements are more ambiguous than others. The degree of ambiguity in a statement is immediately apparent, and in fact it can be definitely measured. The steeper the curve, the smaller is the range of the scale over which it was classified by the readers and the clearer and more precise is the statement. The more gentle the slope of the curve, the more ambiguous is the statement. A simple method of measuring ambiguity is to determine the scale-distance between the scale-value at which the curve of proportions has an ordinate of 0.25 and the scale-value at which the same curve has an ordinate of 0.75. This is merely the quartile distance.

The ambiguity, or Q-value, constitutes one of the objective criteria for eliminating unsuitable statements. Other things being equal, a statement with high Q-value should be eliminated from the scale. It has not been possible to select the statements for the final scale so as to satisfy completely all of the criteria simultaneously but the selection was made with the several criteria listed for each statement.

Since the Q-value is to be used for eliminating ambiguous

statements it becomes a matter of some importance to know if the average Q-value changes for different parts of the scale. In order to make this relation apparent we have plotted the average Q-value against scale-values in Figure 9. This diagram simply means that all the statements with scale-values $0-1$ have an average Q-value of 1.75, and similarly for the other points in the diagram. If all the statements throughout the whole range were

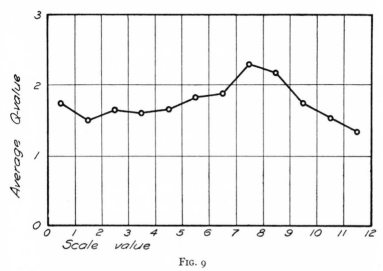

FIG. 9

of the same average ambiguity, the line of this diagram would be horizontal and that would be the ideal condition for our present purposes. It does not show any gross variation in ambiguity although the statements which are in the vicinity of 7 or 8 on the scale have noticeably higher ambiguity than the other statements.

AN OBJECTIVE CRITERION OF IRRELEVANCE

We have tried to devise objective checks on our procedures wherever possible, and in the present experiments we have even retained intentionally a number of statements of opinion which were clearly ambiguous or otherwise unsuitable for an attitude scale in order to see to what extent they could be eliminated by objective methods. We should hardly expect to be able to construct a workable attitude scale entirely by the mechanical application of objective rules. Some latitude will probably always be given to the judgment of the investigator, but our methods will be successful to the extent that the individual judgments of an investigator about material of this sort can be checked objectively. In the present study we retained some material which would have been eliminated by inspection at the very start just in order to test the validity of the several objective criteria.

The criterion of ambiguity is concerned with the spread of a statement over the subjective scale of equal-appearing intervals. If the 300 subjects place a statement of opinion in widely different intervals on the subjective scale, the Q-value of the statement will be large and the statement will therefore be judged by this objective criterion to be ambiguous. It has widely different meanings along the attitude scale when it is read by different subjects. Clearly such statements should be eliminated. Often it is possible to tell by inspection that a statement will have a large Q-value. It should be noted that the Q-value of a statement of opinion does not reflect the actual opinions held by the subjects on the issue in question. They sort the statements merely in accordance with the attitude that they read into the statements without thereby expressing their own attitudes.

The criterion of irrelevance, on the other hand, is concerned with the records of actual votes. The whole list of 130 statements was mimeographed and presented to 300 subjects with the request that they check the statements that they indorsed or agreed with and that they leave blank the statements which they did not care to indorse. It was then possible to study the returns for internal consistency. If we find considerable inconsistency, we might attribute it to the carelessness of the subjects in making their check marks more or less at random, or we might attribute it to defects in the statements themselves. In the present experiments we ound a certain amount of inconsistency throughout the whole list, and it can undoubtedly be attributed at least in part to the subjects themselves. But the inconsistencies vary with the statement that is chosen as a basis of comparison with all the rest, and such differences are due primarily no doubt to defects in the statements themselves. We have so regarded them and we have devised a criterion of irrelevance which can be used further to eliminate the unsuitable statements from the scale.

This criterion is constructed as follows: Suppose that a statement of low ambiguity is properly scaled at the point 6. If a subject has an attitude which is also scaled properly at the point 6, then we should expect him to check that statement. Another subject who is scaled at the point 12 should be less likely to check that statement, and similarly there should be a low probability that a subject at the point zero will check the statement at 6 on the scale.

In order to make this type of analysis quantitative we have devised a rather crude index of similarity which is based on the voting of any large group of subjects. The index of similarity for any pair of statements is based on three facts, namely, n_a = the total number of subjects who indorse statement a in the comparison; n_b = the total number of subjects who indorse statement b in the comparison; n_{ab} = the total number of subjects who indorse both a and b.

If the two statements a and b are practically identical in the attitudes they reflect, then we should expect to find that those subjects who indorse statement a will also indorse statement b. This factor, n_{ab}, will therefore be in the numerator of the index of similarity. On the other hand, the statements vary considerably in intrinsic popularity even when they are scaled at identical points on the scale. The more popular a statement is, the larger will be the number of people who indorse it and any other statement. In order to reduce the index of similarity to the same basis of popularity for all statements, the number of subjects who indorse both statements is divided by the product of the number of total indorsements for each of the two statements so that the index of similarity becomes

$$\frac{n_{ab}}{n_a \cdot n_b}.$$

If we tabulate the indices for statement a with each of all the other statements in turn, we shall have the common factor $1/n_a$ which may be disregarded since it is a constant. We shall then have

Index of similarity[1] for statement $a = C_a = \dfrac{n_{ab}}{n_b}$.

This index is written for the comparison of statement a with each of the others. It is evident that the maximum possible value for this index is unity and its minimum value is zero. If all of the people who indorse statement a also indorse statement k, then the index of similarity is unity as it should be because the two statements are then evidently very similar in the attitudes reflected. If, on the other hand, none of those who indorse statement a also indorse statement k, then the index is zero and this is reasonable because the two statements are then evidently very different in the attitudes which they describe.

In Figure 10 we have a graphical representation of the indices of similarity for statement 96 with each of the other statements, plotted against the scale-value of each statement. The scale-value of statement 96 is indicated by the small arrow on the top line of the diagram. Its index of similarity with itself under ideal conditions would be unity. It is immediately apparent that the indices for statement 96 and each of the other statements are very low for those statements which are distant from statement 96. This is to be expected. In other words, those who indorsed statement 96,

---

[1] Since the completion of this monograph the index of similarity has been developed in a better and more correct form. Its complete description will be published shortly.

which is scaled at 10.5, do not often indorse statements which are scaled in the four or five class-intervals at the other end of the scale. The indices are higher when the second statement approaches the scale-value of statement 96. Every small circle in this diagram represents the index of similarity between statement 96 and a second statement, and it is placed immediately above the scale-value of that second statement.

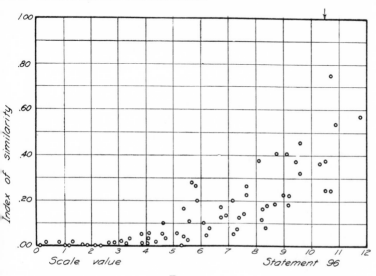

FIG. 10

The criterion of irrelevance is the appearance of the whole diagram. If the indices of similarity are relatively high near the scale-value of the first or common statement and relatively low for statements that are distant from the first or common statement, then the first statement is considered to be satisfactory. It means merely that the people who indorse statement 96 are not so likely to indorse statements that are scaled distant from the scale-value of 96. The appearance of Figure 10 is considered to be satisfactory and therefore statement 96 is retained.

We may turn next to a similar analysis for a statement that

was discarded by the criterion of irrelevance. Figure 11 shows the
indices of similarity for statement 23. The scale-value of this statement is also indicated by a small arrow on the top line of the diagram. Consider the small circle to the extreme left of this diagram.
It is the index of similarity between statement 23 and statement
101, which has a scale-value of 0.02. The index is 0.56. The other
circles are located in a similar manner and represent the degree of

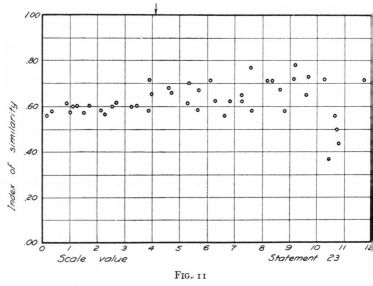

FIG. 11

similarity between statement 23 and each of the other statements.

Note that the people who indorse statement 23 are just as
likely to indorse statements at either extreme of the scale as the
statements that are scaled near to statement 23. The points scatter more or less horizontally on the diagram. This indicates clearly that there is something fundamentally wrong with statement 23
as an index of a particular attitude on the scale. In other words,
if a man indorses this statement we can say nothing about his attitude toward the church because he is likely to indorse not only
statements in the class-interval 4–5 but also at either or both ex-

tremes of the scale as far as one can judge by statement 23. The indorsement of this statement therefore does not help us in allocating the subject to a point on the scale.

We then turn back to the original statement and we find that it reads as follows: "I am interested in a church that is beautiful and that emphasizes the aesthetic side of life." We can now see why this statement is irrelevant to the attitude variable that we are attempting to measure. The pious church-member can certainly indorse this statement conscientiously. Of course he is interested in a church that is beautiful. But the most outspoken atheist can also indorse the statement because he may very well be interested in beautiful buildings, including beautiful churches, and he may very well also be interested in church music even though he does not take at all seriously the religious functions of the church. The attitude reflected by the indorsement of statement 23 is therefore not valid as an index of the attitude variable which is implied in the list of statements as a whole. The fact that the indices of Figure 11 spread more or less horizontally across the whole scale constitutes the objective reason for discarding statement 23.

We may now review more briefly a few additional specimens showing the criterion of irrelevance for other statements. In Figure 12 the indices of similarity have been plotted for statement 7. This statement is scaled at 8.2 and the indices fall to very low values at the other end of the scale. This statement is therefore retained in the final scale.

Figure 13 shows a similar plot for statement 113 in which the indices of similarity fall to rather low values for second statements in the upper half of the scale. The indices are all above 0.90 for the first few class-intervals. The statement is therefore retained for the final scale.

Figure 14 contains a similar plot for statement 49. Here again the indices spread more or less horizontally across the whole scale and therefore statement 49 is discarded. We turn to the original

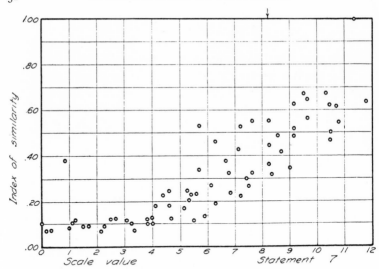

FIG. 12

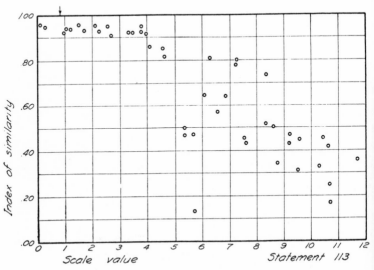

FIG. 13

tatement. It reads as follows: "I do not think one has to belong o the church to be religious." It is quite possible for a pious hurch-member to indorse this statement. It also is possible for he non-religious person to indorse it as a statement of fact even hough he may have no interest in either the church or in religion. t is to be expected that the proportion of indorsements of this

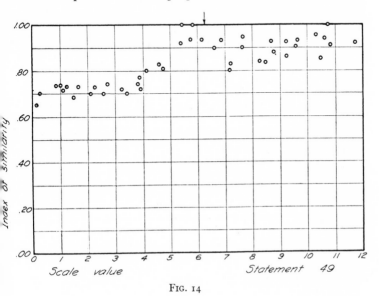

FIG. 14

statement should be higher at the anti-end of the scale and this is what we find in Figure 14, but the discrimination is by no means sufficient. The indices have roughly the same level clear across the scale and the statement is therefore discarded.

Figure 15 shows a satisfactory discrimination for statement 50 because the indices are above 0.90 in the vicinity of the scale-value of statement 50, indicated by the small arrow, and they fall to rather low values at the other end of the scale. The statement is therefore retained.

Figure 16 shows the plot for statement 9, which is discarded

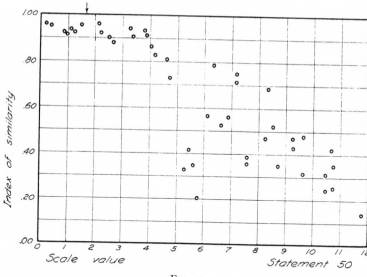

FIG. 15

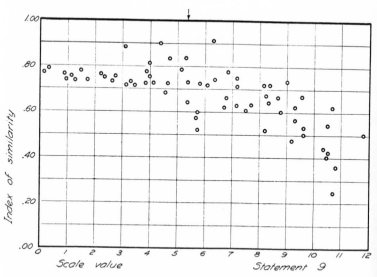

FIG. 16

because the indices of similarity do not show sufficient variation for the different parts of the scale. The statement actually reads: "I don't believe church-going will do anyone any harm." Here again we can readily imagine that the pious church-member will acknowledge the truth of the statement. The strong antichurch voter may also be willing to acknowledge that church-going will not do anyone any harm. The latter group do not so readily indorse the statement as the former, but inspection of the diagram indicates clearly that the discrimination is unsatisfactory. People all over the scale indorse this statement although they may have quite different feelings or ideas in doing so. The mere indorsement of this statement does not help us in locating the voter on the scale. The statement is therefore judged to be irrelevant to the scale, which is represented by the whole list of statements.

It would undoubtedly be possible to quantify the criterion of irrelevance still further. It seems better to delay further quantification until a more generalized rational formulation has been completed.

We have brought to bear on the selection and allocation of the statements of opinion two objective criteria, namely the criterion of ambiguity, the Q-value, which is based on the degree of uniformity in the sorting of the statements, and the criterion of irrelevance, which is based on the consistency of the actual voting, or indorsing. These two parts of our experiments were carried out on two different groups of subjects.

We have found that a statement may be sorted quite uniformly by all the subjects and still be declared unsuitable by the criterion of irrelevance. This may be explained as follows: When we read a statement and then judge the attitude which it would ordinarily represent, we may agree fairly well and thereby assign a low Q-value to the statement. When we are asked to indorse the statement, we may find that people of widely different attitudes find widely different reasons for indorsing it. This is especially likely to happen when a statement can be read either as an expression of attitude or as an expression of fact. For example, the churchman is not likely to volunteer the statement, "Church-going will not do anyone any harm." A person who volunteers that statement spontaneously is not likely to be a devoted church-man. The situation is quite different when the statement is made by someone else and presented for indorsement as to whether it is true or false. In such a situation the churchman may acknowledge the statement to be true even though he would not naturally so express his own attitudes. This distinction between that which we say spontaneously in expressing our attitudes and that which we are willing to acknowledge or indorse when stated by someone else probably accounts for the fact that the criterion of ambiguity and the criterion of irrelevance do not always eliminate the same statements.

Ideally, the scale should perhaps be constructed by means of the voting only. It may be possible to formulate the problem so that the scale values of the statements may be extracted from the records of actual voting. If that should be possible, then the present procedure of establishing the scale-values by sorting will be superseded.

INFORMAL CRITERIA FOR THE SELECTION OF OPINIONS

As a result of our work on the present attitude scale we have formulated a list of informal criteria which will be used in the construction of future attitude scales. By these criteria it is seen that many of the opinions in the present experimental scale are defective, and it is our plan to start the construction of an improved attitude scale which shall be free as far as possible from the defects that we can now describe, but these criteria were not clearly formulated when the original material for the present experiments was compiled.

The following is a list of some informal criteria for the selection of opinions in the construction of an attitude scale. The list is certainly not complete and it may very well be decided that some of the following characteristics are not defects.

1. As far as possible, the opinions should reflect the present attitude of the subject rather than his attitudes in the past. By wording the opinions in the present tense one avoids the situation in which a subject might indorse two conflicting opinions, one referring to his past attitude and one to his present attitude. The scale-value of the subject should naturally describe his present attitude.

2. It has been found that double-barreled statements tend to be ambiguous. The material should be edited so that each opinion expresses as far as possible only one thought or idea. The subject is confused in reading a double statement in which he might want to indorse one idea but not the other. Example: "I believe in the ideals of the church but I am tired of denominationalism." Perhaps this statement would serve better if it were divided into two opinions.

3. One should avoid statements which are evidently applicable to a very restricted range of indorsers. Example: "I go to church because I enjoy good music. I am in the choir and get musical training and chorus-singing." The first sentence can be indorsed by a fairly wide group of indorsers, but the second statement can be indorsed only by those who happen to be members of a church choir. It is probably not worth while to include opinions which are so restricted by factual qualifications in an attitude scale. What we want to measure is attitude and in doing so we should avoid so marked an influence on the range of possible indorsers. The foregoing statement would probably be much improved for our purposes if only the first sentence were retained for scaling.

4. Each opinion selected for the attitude scale should preferably be such that it is not possible for subjects from both ends of the scale to indorse it. Such opinions will be canceled by the objective criteria, but when this defect is conspicuous the state-

ment might as well be discarded at the start. On the other hand, there will probably always be a certain number of opinions in a list which have this defect and which are not recognized when read by the investigator. Later, when they are discarded by the objective criteria it is usually easy to see why it is that these statements are eliminated. In other words, it is easier to have the objective basis for discarding a statement and then to see why it should have been discarded by inspection than to spot these defective statements in the reading of the original whole list of statements.

5. As far as possible the statements should be free from related and confusing concepts. In the present material we have a number of statements which mention "true religion" and "the religion of Jesus." These statements are likely to be difficult to interpret because, in addition to the assertions about the church, these statements involve also additional though related concepts which might as well be avoided wherever possible. Example: "I think the church allows denominational differences to appear larger than true religion." A statement of this type can just as well be written directly with reference to the alleged overemphasis of denominational differences by the churches without involving the uncertainties of interpretation of the phrase, "true religion."

6. Other things being equal, slang may be avoided except where it serves the purpose of describing an attitude more briefly than it could otherwise be stated. For example, to say that most sermons are "all bunk" may be justified if it should be considered a natural way of expressing an attitude which is to be represented on the scale.

CHAPTER IV
THE EXPERIMENTAL ATTITUDE SCALE
DESCRIPTION OF THE SCALE

A final list of 45 statements of opinion was selected from the original list of 130 opinions. The selection was made with consideration of the criterion of ambiguity, the criterion of irrelevance, the scale-values, and by inspection of the statements. The statements were so selected that they constitute a more or less uniformly graduated series of scale-values. The scale-values represented by the 45 statements in the final list are shown in Figure 17, the purpose of which is to show that the 45 statements repre-

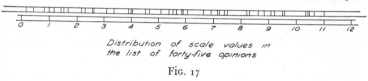

Distribution of scale values in the list of forty-five opinions

Fig. 17

sent a more or less evenly graduated series of scale-values. The two upper horizontal lines constitute the scale proper and between these two lines there are small cross lines. Each of these cross lines represents the location of one of the 45 opinions. There are forty-five such cross lines. The class intervals on the scale and their numerical designations are indicated immediately below. Inspection of the figure shows that the graduation is by no means perfect but it is probably as close as is necessary. Four opinions were selected from each of the eleven class-intervals of the scale. In addition, one extreme statement that scaled at 11.8 or beyond was included.

The experimental scale as finally presented to the several hundred subjects for actual voting together with the accompanying instructions is given here. The questions on the title page of the blank were inserted for the possibility of correlating facts obtained from the replies with the scores on the attitude scale. For our present purposes these items are of secondary importance although in the practical use of a scale of this kind these correlational items probably would constitute an essential part of the investigation. As a by-product of our present investigation, we have tabulated the various facts about the voters in order that separate frequency distributions may be constructed for subjects of various classifications.

EXPERIMENTAL STUDY OF ATTITUDE
TOWARD THE CHURCH

This is an experimental study of the distribution of attitude toward the church. You will be asked to read a list of statements about the church and to indorse those that express your own sentiment. Let your own experience with churches determine your indorsements.

1. Name*_____

2. Group_____

3. Underline your classification:
   Freshman, Sophomore, Junior, Senior, Graduate, Faculty, Unclassified

4. Department of major work:_____

5. Do you attend church frequently? Yes   No   (Underline one)

6. Are you an active member of a church? Yes   No   (Underline one)

7. Before turning this page write a brief statement indicating your general attitude toward the church as you know it.

_____

_____

8. Write an × somewhere on the line below to indicate where you think you belong.

_____

| Strongly favorable | Neutral | Strongly against |
| to the church | | the church |

* You need not sign your name, if you prefer to give your opinions anonymously.

Check ($\sqrt{}$) every statement below that expresses your sentiment toward the church. Interpret the statements in accordance with your own experience with churches.[1]

(40)   1. I think the teaching of the church is altogether too superficial to have much social significance.

(50)   2. I feel the church services give me inspiration and help me to live up to my best during the following week.

(110)   3. I think the church keeps business and politics up to a higher standard than they would otherwise tend to maintain.

(103)   4. I find the services of the church both restful and inspiring.

(54)   5. When I go to church I enjoy a fine ritual service with good music.

(28)   6. I believe in what the church teaches but with mental reservations.

(77)   7. I do not receive any benefit from attending church services but I think it helps some people.

(13)   8. I believe in religion but I seldom go to church.

(69)   9. I am careless about religion and church relationships but I would not like to see my attitude become general.

(96)   10. I regard the church as a static, crystallized institution and as such it is unwholesome and detrimental to society and the individual.

(93)   11. I believe church membership is almost essential to living life at its best.

(21)   12. I do not understand the dogmas or creeds of the church but I find that the church helps me to be more honest and creditable.

(7)   13. The paternal and benevolent attitude of the church is quite distasteful to me.

(19)   14. I feel that church attendance is a fair index of the nation's morality.

(34)   15. Sometimes I feel that the church and religion are necessary and sometimes I doubt it.

(114)   16. I believe the church is fundamentally sound but some of its adherents have given it a bad name.

(65)   17. I think the church is a parasite on society.

[1] The statements of this list are numbered consecutively as shown. The number in parentheses before each statement refers to the original list of 130 statements.

(64)   18. I feel the need for religion but do not find what I want in any one church.

(38)   19. I think too much money is being spent on the church for the benefit that is being derived.

(11)   20. I believe in the church and its teachings because I have been accustomed to them since I was a child.

(87)   21. I think the church is hundreds of years behind the times and cannot make a dent on modern life.

(89)   22. I believe the church has grown up with the primary purpose of perpetuating the spirit and teachings of Jesus and deserves loyal support.

(113)   23. I feel the church perpetuates the values which man puts highest in his philosophy of life.

(51)   24. I feel I can worship God better out of doors than in the church and I get more inspiration there.

(128)   25. My experience is that the church is hopelessly out of date.

(33)   26. I feel the church is petty, always quarreling over matters that have no interest or importance.

(95)   27. I do not believe in any brand of religion or in any particular church but I have never given the subject serious thought.

(125)   28. I respect any church-member's beliefs but I think it is all "bunk."

(74)   29. I enjoy my church because there is a spirit of friendliness there.

(41)   30. I think the country would be better off if the churches were closed and the ministers set to some useful work.

(101)   31. I believe the church is the greatest institution in America today.

(27)   32. I believe in sincerity and goodness without any church ceremonies.

(75)   33. I believe the church is the greatest influence for good government and right living.

(72)   34. I think the organized church is an enemy of science and truth.

(56)   35. I believe the church is losing ground as education advances.

(24)   36. The churches may be doing good and useful work but they do not interest me.

(110)   37. I think the church is a hindrance to religion for it still depends upon magic, superstition, and myth.

(107)   38. The church is needed to develop religion, which has always been concerned with man's deepest feelings and greatest values.

(36)   39. I believe the churches are too much divided by factions and denominations to be a strong force for righteousness.

(48)   40. The church represents shallowness, hypocrisy, and prejudice.

(127)   41. I think the church seeks to impose a lot of worn-out dogmas and
medieval superstitions.

(14)   42. I think the church allows denominational differences to appear
larger than true religion.

(90)   43. I like the ceremonies of my church but do not miss them much
when I stay away.

(100)   44. I believe the church is a powerful agency for promoting both individual and social righteousness.

(73)   45. I like to go to church for I get something worth while to think
about and it keeps my mind filled with right thoughts.

METHOD OF SCORING

We have given numerical designations to the successive class-
intervals of the scale. The unit of measurement is defined by the
number of equal-appearing intervals into which the original list
of 130 statements was sorted by the first group of subjects. Since
the subjects were asked to sort out the 130 statements into eleven
piles subjectively equally distant from each other, the unit of
measurement is thereby defined. The origin is arbitrarily assigned. We could have placed the origin in the middle of the
scale, but that would necessitate dealing with negative class-intervals and nothing is statistically gained thereby. We therefore assigned the origin to one end of the scale, the extreme pro-end. In
most mental tests the high and low scores represent performances
that can be described as good or bad, but in the present instance
there is, of course, no such possibility. We have no right to say
that a person who is very much devoted to his church is in any
sense better than a person who has no such affiliations. Nor can
we say that one person scores "higher" than another except in the
arbitrary sense that one end of the scale is called zero and the
other end eleven. It is a matter of indifference which end is chosen
for the high numerical scores. What we are here concerned with

is merely the description of one aspect of the attitudes of people about the church, an aspect which can be thought of as a linear continuum. We have no interest in any implications that one score is better than some other score in a moral sense or that one score is higher than some other score in the sense of relative value or achievement. These considerations, important for the unbiased construction of an attitude scale, of course leave any user of such a scale entirely free to make his own moral interpretations of the scores.

It is to be expected that many of the users of an attitude scale will have as their motive the influencing of people toward a chosen end of the scale. Our object is to produce a tool, as objective as possible, by which to describe attitudes. In the absence of objective tools for the description of social phenomena, the conclusions of any investigator are always subject to the challenge that he has reported his facts with his own bias, either intentionally or unintentionally. To the extent that social phenomena may be described with devices that are free from the investigator's own bias, to that extent we shall be able to make sound inferences, to just that extent shall we be able to separate our facts from our own personal desires.

Having adopted an origin of measurement which is assigned arbitrarily at one end of the series of available opinions, and having a unit of measurement, the equal-appearing interval as described, we can proceed to ascertain the mean scale-value of all the opinions that any individual subject indorses. This mean scale-value of all the opinions which a subject indorses we call his *score*.

In the clerical work of scoring the blanks there are two alternative procedures which will probably give substantially the same results. We may assign the scale-value to each of the statements that a subject has indorsed and then calculate their arithmetic mean. This is legitimate to the extent that each class-interval of the scale is equally represented by opinions. Since we have the 45 statements in the experimental scale graduated more or less evenly, we feel justified in allocating each subject to the scale at the mean scale-value of the opinions that he has indorsed. This seems reasonable because there is approximately the same number of opinions available for him to check in each class-interval.

Another procedure which is statistically equivalent is to assign a rank order number to each of the 45 statements in the scale and merely to calculate the average rank order of the statements which he has indorsed. This procedure is equivalent to the previous method in so far as we have the 45 opinions evenly spaced throughout the scale. In the blank the 45 statements were presented in random order, not in the order of their scale-values. This was done in order to encourage the subject to read all of the statements.

RELIABILITY OF THE SCORE

In order to test the reliability of the experimental scale it was divided into two parts. The usual procedure of assigning alternate items to the two forms A and B was slightly modified because that procedure would give one of the two parallel forms a slightly higher mean scale-value than the other. In order to make the two forms truly parallel, as far as that was possible with the material at hand, we arranged all the opinions of the scale in rank order according to their scale-values. Successive pairs were then marked off. The first opinion in each pair had, of course, a slightly lower scale-value than the second. In the odd numbered pairs the first opinion with the lower scale-value was assigned to form A of the scale, and in the even numbered pairs the second opinion with the higher scale-value was assigned to form A of the test. The others were assigned to form B. In this manner we obtained two forms, A and B, each half as long as the experimental scale, and so prepared that the average scale-values of the two forms were practically identical. The odd statement scaled at 11.8 was included in both forms, A and B.

The blanks of two hundred Freshmen were used for the purpose of determining reliability. Each blank was given two scores, one score for the opinions that had been assigned to form A and a second score from the same blank for the opinions that had been assigned to form B. The two sets of two hundred partial scores were then correlated. The correlation between the two sets of scores was 0.848. When this correlation between the two halves of the scale is interpreted by means of the Spearman-Brown formula, the estimated reliability of the whole scale is 0.92, which is quite satisfactory. Earlier in the study the same procedure was applied to the blanks of one hundred subjects in which the correlation between the two halves of the scale turned out to be 0.89, which is comparable with the correlation of 0.85 between the two halves of the scale for the larger group of two hundred subjects. If the correlation of 0.89 between the two halves for the one hundred subjects is interpreted by the Spearman-Brown formula, the reliability of the whole test is estimated to be 0.94.

CHAPTER V

APPLICATION OF THE EXPERIMENTAL SCALE

SOME ACTUAL DISTRIBUTIONS OF ATTITUDE

While the scale developed in these experiments cannot be regarded as completely satisfactory, it is sufficiently diagnostic to make it worth trying on several groups for comparative purposes.

TABLE IV

DISTRIBUTION OF ATTITUDE IN SEVERAL GROUPS

SCALE	FRESHMEN		SOPHO-MORES		JUNIORS		SENIORS		GRADUATE STUDENTS		DIVINITY STUDENTS		CHICAGO FORUM	
	f*	p	f	p	f	p	f	p	f	p	f	p	f	p
0– 0.9...	....	.....	..	.....	..	.....	..	.....	..	.....	..	.....	..	.....
1– 1.9...	52	.095	1	.008	10	.093	2	.019	10	.048	17	.165	23	.127
2– 2.9...	129	.236	24	.189	22	.206	24	.224	49	.234	52	.504	28	.155
3– 3.9...	92	.168	23	.182	15	.140	19	.178	36	.171	24	.233	14	.077
4– 4.9...	69	.126	17	.134	15	.140	16	.150	29	.138	5	.049	17	.094
5– 5.9...	62	.113	16	.126	15	.140	13	.121	13	.c62	4	.039	15	.083
6– 6.9...	69	.126	24	.189	14	.132	17	.159	26	.124	1	.010	20	.110
7– 7.9...	43	.078	14	.110	10	.093	10	.093	24	.114	...	.....	26	.144
8– 8.9...	27	.049	4	.031	6	.056	4	.037	15	.071	...	.....	28	.155
9– 9.9...	5	.009	4	.031	...	.....	2	.019	5	.024	...	.....	10	.055
10–10.9...	...	.....	...	.....	...	.....	...	.....	3	.014	...	.....	...	.....
Total...	548	1.000	127	1.000	107	1.000	107	1.000	210	1.000	103	1.000	181	1.000
Average	4.42		5.04		4.57		4.78		4.86		2.82		5.36	

* f = frequency, p = proportion.

The scale was presented to students at the University of Chicago, both undergraduates and graduates, to some faculty members, and to the Chicago Forum. In Table IV the frequency distributions of scores are summarized and in Figure 18 these frequency distributions are shown graphically for the groups larger than one hundred subjects. All of these distributions have been reduced to the same area by expressing each class-frequency as a proportion of the entire group.

The mean score for each group is indicated by a small arrow on the base line. Inspection of these frequency polygons shows immediately the wide range of attitude toward the church rep-

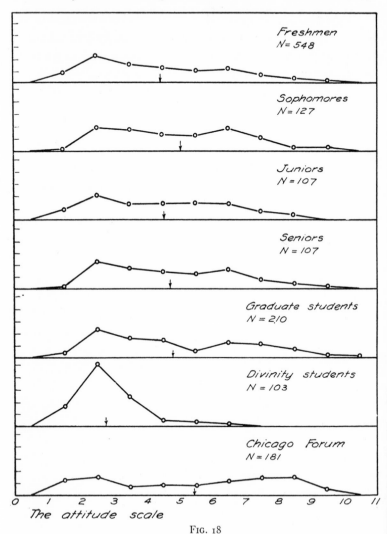

FIG. 18

resented in all these groups. As is to be expected, the divinity students concentrate more strongly in favor of the church than any of the other groups. The Chicago Forum has the highest score, indicating that this group is, on the average, more frankly antagonistic to the church than any of the student groups. The four undergraduate classes do not show any distinct trend to become more in favor of or more against the church as they progress through college. The graduate students score about the same, on the average, as the undergraduate students. Our groups may not be large enough and our scale may not be sufficiently perfected to make these conclusions final.

TABLE V

DISPERSION OF ATTITUDE SCORES

	Standard Deviation of Scores
Freshmen	2.07
Sophomores	1.93
Juniors	2.02
Seniors	1.93
Graduate students	2.27
Divinity students	0.96
Chicago Forum	2.56

The several distributions represented in Figure 18 vary somewhat in the dispersion of scores. In Table V the standard deviations are listed for the several distributions of scores on the experimental attitude scale. It will be seen that the dispersion of scores is approximately the same for the four undergraduate classes. The variability in attitude increases for the graduate students. The divinity students have the smallest scatter and the sample of 183 records from the Chicago Forum shows the widest scatter in attitude toward the church.

As a tentative application of the experimental scale, we have tabulated the frequency distributions for several groups which might conceivably differ in their attitudes toward the church. In

Figure 19 we have the distributions for Jews, Protestants, and Catholics. Inspection of the distributions shows immediately that

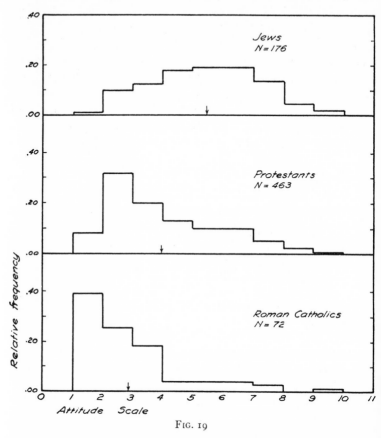

Fig. 19

the Catholics are as a whole most strongly favorable toward the church. The Jews are as a whole more indifferent and more frequently antagonistic toward the church. The Protestants occupy an intermediate position on the scale. These results are probably what we should expect. The actual frequencies with the arithmetic mean for each distribution are summarized in Table VI.

It should be noted that in drawing these frequency distributions we have reduced the areas of all the surfaces to unity. Each ordinate is therefore expressed in terms of relative frequency, i.e., the proportion of the whole distribution that is found in a class-interval. In this manner the sum of the relative frequencies for all the class-intervals must equal unity for each distribution. The purpose of this reduction is to facilitate the comparison of the dis-

TABLE VI

FREQUENCY DISTRIBUTIONS OF ATTITUDE TOWARD THE CHURCH

CLASS-INTERVAL	ROMAN CATHOLIC		PROTESTANT		JEW		MEN		WOMEN		CHURCH ATTENDANCE				ACTIVE CHURCH-MEMBER			
											Yes		No		Yes		No	
0– 1	..	..	..	..	..	..	..	..	..	..	..	..	..	..	..	..	..	..
1– 2	28	.389	37	.080	2	.011	49	.080	55	.131	119	.176	6	.009	106	.182	13	.017
2– 3	19	.264	149	.322	17	.097	167	.273	101	.241	282	.416	40	.058	245	.422	81	.104
3– 4	13	.181	92	.199	22	.125	95	.155	74	.177	155	.229	75	.108	114	.196	106	.136
4– 5	3	.042	58	.125	31	.176	67	.109	52	.124	66	.097	98	.142	54	.093	106	.136
5– 6	3	.042	47	.102	34	.193	64	.105	39	.093	30	.044	120	.173	33	.057	108	.138
6– 7	3	.042	44	.095	33	.187	57	.093	50	.119	15	.022	148	.214	20	.034	139	.178
7– 8	2	.028	25	.054	24	.136	58	.095	31	.074	7	.010	100	.145	7	.012	116	.149
8– 9	0	.000	10	.022	9	.051	42	.069	13	.031	4	.006	81	.117	2	.003	84	.108
9–10	1	.014	1	.002	4	.023	11	.018	3	.007	..	..	22	.032	..	..	26	.033
10–11	..	..	..	..	..	..	2	.003	1	.002	..	..	2	.003	..	..	2	.003
Total	72	1.002	463	1.001	176	.999	612	1.000	419	.999	678	1.000	692	1.001	581	.999	781	1.002
Average scale-value	2.9027		3.9687		5.4432		4.5180		4.1754		3.0560		5.9292		3.0886		5.6588	

tributions as to relative range and the location of the central tendency. If the distributions were drawn with the actual frequencies, they would of course be different in average height owing to the variation in the total number of cases in the several distributions. This might be a distraction in the inspection and comparison of the diagrams. The actual frequencies, are, however, presented in Table VI. In each of these frequency diagrams the arithmetic mean is represented by a small arrow on the base line. Its numerical value will be found in Table VI.

In Figure 20 we have a graphical comparison of men and women. These two frequency surfaces have been drawn in the same manner as the preceding diagram. The spread is comparable for men and for women. The arithmetic means indicate that on the whole perhaps the women are slightly more favorable to the

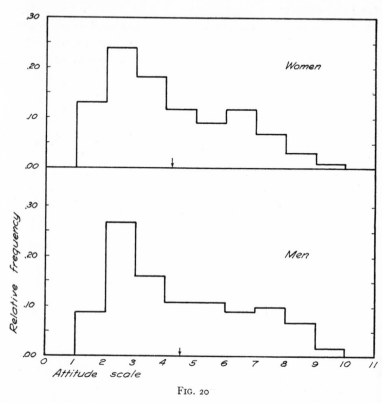

FIG. 20

church than the men. The present distributions are drawn primarily in order to illustrate the manner of using an attitude scale.

On the title page of the printed form of the experimental scale we asked each subject whether or not he attended church frequently. The subjects who answered this question were divided into two groups according to whether their answer to this question was "yes" or "no." These two distributions of attitude are shown in Figure 21. The two groups are comparable in size. It will be seen that there is a rather striking difference in the mean scale position of those who attend church frequently and of those who do not. This is, of course, as one would expect.

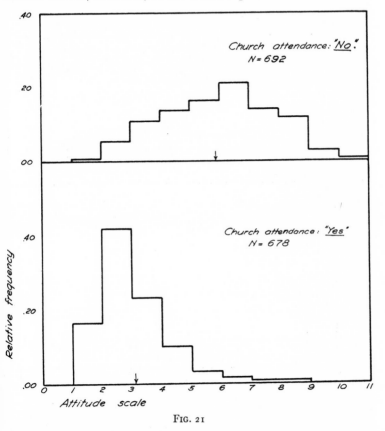

FIG. 21

A similar difference is seen in Figure 22 between the attitudes of those who are active church-members and those who are not. These frequency distributions reveal nothing that would not be expected beforehand, but they indicate at least that the scale does not give absurd results when applied to situations about which we

can make a reasonable prediction. If the scale gives reasonable results in those groups whose attitudes toward the church are known
beforehand it is a fair inference that the same scale might be used
with some assurance in measuring the attitudes of groups about
which we cannot make predictions.

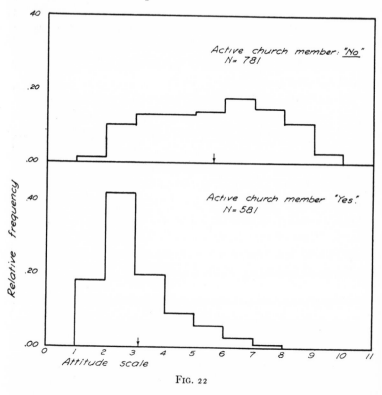

FIG. 22

The validity of the unit of measurement for the attitude scale
is not demonstrated by these frequency distributions. It is conceivable that results as differentiating as these might be obtained
even if the scale consisted of nothing more than a series of statements arranged in rank order and numbered serially. To es-
tablish the validity of the unit of measurement is one of the most

important problems in the measurement of attitude. It can be done perhaps best by asking two groups of individuals who are known to differ in their attitude on the issue in question to sort a series of one hundred or more statements into the eleven piles. The scale-values should be ascertained independently for the two groups. Now if the two scales so produced give substantially the same scale-values for the statements, then we shall have experimental evidence that the attitudes of the people who sort the statements have a negligible effect on the scale itself. Such an experiment is now under way.

The method of equal-appearing intervals is used here not without realizing its limitations. It has been used in the measurement of handwriting excellence and of other educational products without admission by the authors that the scale-values so obtained might not be valid. It is likely that the scale-values are somewhat less valid than those obtained by the method of paired comparison or its equivalent. I know of no published study of the discrepancies in scale-values of educational products calculated by the two methods. Some crucial experiments to determine the validity of the method of equal-appearing intervals are now under way in the psychological laboratory of the University of Chicago.

ALTERNATIVE FORMS OF THE FREQUENCY DISTRIBUTIONS

One of our principal objectives in the measurement of attitude is to plot a frequency distribution of attitude which shall be descriptive of a group. A high ordinate of such a frequency distribution should indicate that the attitude represented by that part of the scale is relatively popular in the group in question and, similarly, a low ordinate should indicate that the attitude represented by that part of the scale is relatively unpopular in the particular group.

There are at least two different methods by which these frequency distributions may be plotted, and they are both illustrated in Figure 23 for the same group and for the same scale. It is of course possible to tabulate a frequency distribution of scores and to represent this distribution graphically. This is shown in the

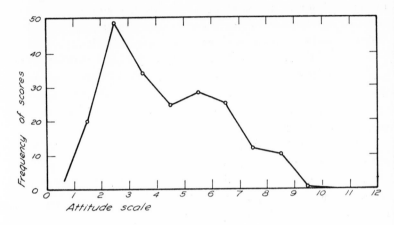

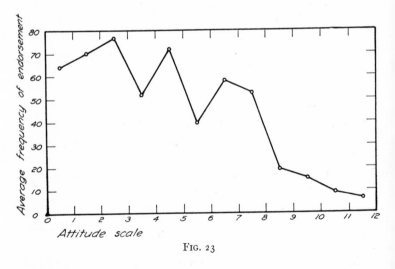

Fig. 23

upper part of Figure 23. The area of such a diagram represents the total number of individuals in the group, and the ordinate for any particular class-interval represents the actual number of individuals whose scores fall in that class-interval. The interpretation of such a frequency polygon is relatively simple.

Another method is to calculate the average number of indorsements per statement in each class-interval and to plot a distribution with these values as ordinates. The area of such a frequency diagram will be proportional to the number of indorsements made by the whole group to all of the statements in the scale if the opinions in the scale are evenly graduated. This type of distribution is shown in the lower part of Figure 23 for the same group and for the same scale.

The numerical values from which the two diagrams of Figure 23 were plotted are shown in Table VII. In the first column are recorded the scale values of the respective statements. In the second column are listed the code numbers of the statements. The third column shows the total number of indorsements for each of the statements in a group of 203 University of Chicago Freshmen whose papers were drawn at random from the total of 548 records specially for the purpose of comparing these two types of frequency distributions. For example, the first line of Table VII shows that statement 31 has a scale value of 0.2 and that it was given 50 indorsements by the present group of 203 freshmen. The first entry in the fourth column shows that the average number of indorsements per statement in the first class-interval was 64.4. It is merely the average of the entries 50, 61, and 82. The second entry of the last column shows that there were 20 students in the present group whose scores on the scale were between 1 and 2. The rest of the table is interpreted in the same manner. The upper part of Figure 23 is plotted directly from the last column of Table VII, and the lower diagram is plotted from the entries in the fourth column of the table.

It would seem that either of these two methods of drawing the frequency distribution of attitude might be justified. One of them shows the frequency distribution of individual scores with a total

TABLE VII

SCALING RECORD FOR A GROUP OF 203 UNIVERSITY OF CHICAGO FRESHMEN

Scale-Value	Statement No.	Total Number of Indorsements	Average Number of Indorsements per Statement	Total Number of Scores
0.2........	31	50	....	....
0.4........	33	61	....	....
0.8........	23	82	64.4	0
1.0........	22	69	....	....
1.2........	44	60	....	....
1.4........	38	77	....	....
1.5........	11	60	....	....
1.7........	2	84	70.0	20
2.2........	45	75	....	....
2.3........	4	101	....	....
2.6........	3	75	....	....
2.6........	14	57	77.0	48
3.1........	12	31	....	....
3.3........	29	66	....	....
3.9...·....	16	58	51.7	34
4.0........	5	85	....	....
4.0........	20	65	....	....
4.5........	6	96	....	....
4.7........	9	40	71.5	25
5.1........	43	40	....	....
5.4........	8	60	....	....
5.6........	15	68	....	....
5.7........	7	34	....	....
5.9........	27	17	....	....
5.9........	36	17	39.4	28
6.1........	18	35	....	....
6.7........:	32	89	....	....
6.9........	24	49	57.8	25
7.2........	39	60	....	....
7.2........	42	53	....	....
7.4........	35	72	....	....
7.5........	19	25	52.5	12
8.2........	13	15	....	....
8.3........	1	24	....	....
8.6........	26	22	....	....
8.8........	28	15	19.0	10
9.1........	25	10	....	....
9.2........	41	13	....	....
9.5........	21	24	....	....
9.6........	37	14	15.2	1

TABLE VII—*Continued*

Scale-Value	Statement No.	Total Number of Indorsements	Average Number of Indorsements per Statement	Total Number of Scores
10.4.........	40	10	....	....
10.5.........	10	6	....	....
10.5.........	30	2	....	....
10.7.........	34	19	9.2	0
11.0.........	17	7	7.0	0
Total....	2,092		203	

area equal to the number of individuals in the group. The other shows the average relative popularity of the statements in each class-interval. The total area of this surface is proportional to the total number of indorsements when the statements are exactly evenly graduated on the scale.

It is clear that the spread of the lower diagram must be greater than the upper diagram of scores because statements may be indorsed even when they are too extreme to constitute any person's score. It is our present belief that the upper diagram shows the preferable way of representing the distribution of attitude in a group. It is perhaps the simpler to explain or to interpret. It is merely the frequency distribution of scores on an attitude scale.

CORRELATION BETWEEN THE ATTITUDE SCORES AND SELF-RATINGS

On the title page of the experimental attitude scale we inserted a graphic rating scale. This scale consists merely of a horizontal line across the page on which we asked the subject to indicate by a cross where he estimated his own attitude to be. At one end of this line was printed the phrase, "Strongly favorable to the church"; at the middle of the line was printed the word "Neutral"; and at the other end of the line there was the phrase "Strongly against the church." Not enough instruction was given

in the use of a self-rating scale to make this record of much consequence, but we included it for what it might be worth.

When the papers were scored for the attitude scale a record
was also made of the tenth of the horizontal line in which the subject had placed a cross to indicate where he estimated his own
attitude to be. It is of course to be expected that there should be
correlation between the score on the attitude scale and the position of the check mark or cross on the self-rating line. The correlation between the score on the attitude scale and the tenth of the
line in which the self-rating check occurred was found to be 0.67,
which is fairly satisfactory.

We have no estimate of the reliability of these self-ratings and
consequently we cannot make any significant inference from this
correlation. Any interpretation would also be subject to the ambiguity that this correlation may be called an index of the validity
of the attitude scale in terms of the self-ratings as a criterion, or
it may be called an index of the validity of the self-ratings in
terms of the attitude scale as a criterion. In either case, taken at
its worst, the correlation between these two indices is closer than
the correlation between most psychological tests and their respective criteria. It was frequently found that a subject would
rate himself as "neutral" on the self-rating line and check most of
the statements strongly against the church in the attitude scale.
This happened very frequently. In fact we believe we are justified
in our inference that a subject will usually call himself slightly
more favorable to the church than is indicated by the actual
statements that he indorses. Perhaps this is because of the social
pressure against the outspoken denial of the institutions that most
people hold in high respect. It may also be that some of our subjects failed to understand the scale and interpreted "neutral" to
mean complete or active indifference to the church.

SUMMARY OF APPLICATIONS

The practical application of the present measurement technique consists in presenting the final list of statements of opinion

to the group to be studied with the request that they check with plus signs all the statements with which they agree and with minus signs all the statements with which they disagree. The score for each person is the average scale-value of all the statements that he has indorsed. In order that the scale be effective toward the extremes, it is advisable that the statements in the scale be extended in both directions considerably beyond the attitudes which will ever be encountered as mean-values for individuals. When the score has been determined for each person by the simple summation just indicated, a frequency distribution can be plotted for the attitudes of any specified group.

The reliability of the scale can be ascertained by preparing two parallel forms from the same material and by presenting both forms to the same individuals. The correlation between the two scores obtained for each person in a group will then indicate the reliability of the scale. Since the heterogeneity of the group affects the reliability coefficient, it is necessary to specify the standard deviation of the scores of the group on which the reliability coefficient is determined. The standard error of an individual score can also be calculated by an analogous procedure.

The unit of measurement in the scale when constructed by the procedure here outlined is not the standard discriminal error projected by a single statement on the psychological continuum. Such a unit of measurement can be obtained by the direct application of the law of comparative judgment, but it is considerably more laborious than the method here described. The unit in the present scale is a more arbitrary one, namely, one-eleventh of the range on the psychological continuum which covers the span from what the readers regard as extreme affirmation to extreme negation in the particular list of statements with which we start. Of course the scale-values can be determined with reliability to fractional parts of this unit. It is hoped that this unit may be shown experimentally to be proportional to a more precise and more universal unit of measurement, such as the standard discriminal error of a single statement of opinion.

It is legitimate to determine a central tendency for the frequency distribution of attitudes in a group. Several groups of individuals may then be compared as regards the means of their respective frequency distributions of attitudes. The differences between the means of several such distributions may be directly compared because of the fact that a rational base line has been established. Such comparisons are not possible when attitudes are ascertained merely by counting the number of indorsements to separate statements whose scale differences have not been measured.

In addition to specifying the mean attitude of each of several groups, it is also possible to measure their relative heterogeneity with regard to the issue in question. Thus it will be possible, by means of our present measurement methods, to discover for example that one group is 1.6 more heterogeneous in its attitudes about prohibition than some other group. The heterogeneity of a group is indicated perhaps best by the standard deviation of the scale-values of all the opinions that have been indorsed by the group as a whole rather than by the standard deviation of the distribution of individual mean scores. Perhaps different terms should be adopted for these two types of measurement.

The tolerance which a person reveals on any particular issue is also subject to quantitative measurement. It is the standard deviation of the scale-values of the statements that he indorses. The maximum possible tolerance is, of course, the indorsement of all the statements throughout the whole range of the scale.

If it is desired to know which of two forms of appeal is the more effective on any particular issue, this can be determined by using the scale before and after the appeal. The difference between the individual scores, before and after, can be tabulated and the average shift in attitude following any specified form of appeal can be measured.

The essential characteristic of the present measurement method is the scale of evenly graduated opinions so arranged that equal steps or intervals on the scale *seem* to most people to represent equally noticeable shifts in attitude.

CHAPTER VI

FURTHER STUDIES OF VALIDITY

In the previous chapter we have already referred to the use of the information obtained from the first page of the test form. These data have been shown to have value in establishing both the reliability and validity of the scale. They will now be further examined to show their significance in the interpretation of the results obtained from our objective measurement of several groups. This double check is of special value when the scale is to be used as a basis of educational program or guidance. The free statements made by each subject on the first page of his blank are useful in the interpretation of the frequency distributions.

These free statements of attitude have also been carefully studied and are being used in the revision of the scale. The attitude variable will be more specifically defined. The title of the scale will probably read, "Attitude toward the Best Type of Church I Know." Experience with the first scale suggests this change in statement and the revision will undoubtedly aid in making a more accurate diagnostic instrument.

On the first page of the blank there were two questions: "Do you attend church frequently?" and "Are you an active member of a church?" Each person was asked before checking the statements of the scale to write a brief statement of his own attitude toward the church. In answer to the first question 50.2 per cent of the Freshmen, 36.7 per cent of the Sophomores, 42.7 per cent of the Juniors, 45.2 per cent of the Seniors, and 46 per cent of the graduates said they attended church frequently. In response to the second question, the percentages of the groups who said they were active members were: Freshmen, 38.2 per cent; Sophomores, 28.1 per cent; Juniors, 36.0 per cent; Seniors, 37.5 per cent, and graduates, 40.2 per cent. In each case there is a distinct drop in percentage from the Freshmen class to the Sophomore class but an increase in percentage from the Sophomore group to the graduates. The largest percentage of frequent attendance is in the Freshmen group, but the largest percentage of active members is in the graduate group. The graduate group was composed chiefly of classes in the law, medical, and psychological departments. The undergraduate groups were of wider samplings.

TABLE VIII

RELATION BY SCORES AND ANSWERS

	SCALE POSITION OF STUDENTS 0–5.0 (FAVORABLE END OF SCALE)		SCALE POSITION OF STUDENTS 5.1–10.9 (ANTICHURCH END OF SCALE)	
	Yes	No	Yes	No
Attend church frequently:				
Freshmen	46.9%	16.7%	3.3%	33.1%
Sophomore	32.1	24.2	4.6	39.1
Junior	38.8	20.4	2.9	37.9
Senior	42.3	19.2	2.9	35.6
Graduate	40.2	19.6	5.7	34.5
Active members:				
Freshmen	35.3	28.3	3.0	33.4
Sophomore	23.4	32.8	4.7	39.1
Junior	32.0	27.2	3.9	36.9
Senior	34.6	26.9	2.9	35.6
Graduate	34.9	24.9	5.3	34.9

Table VIII indicates the relation between the scores on the test and the answers to the two foregoing questions. On the average it was nearly ten to one that if a person voted "yes" on either question of frequent attendance or active membership his scale position would be found in the favorable half of the scale. However, a considerable number who are rated in the antichurch half of the scale indicated the habit of frequent attendance and active membership in the church.

Students rated in every part of the scale showed appreciation of the church as an institution in society. Only a few gave unqualified approval or disapproval. Nearly all marked shortcom-

ngs of the church. The range of statements on the scale indorsed
by members of each group, as indicated by the graphs, was wide,
but there were few at the extremes. Likewise in the written statements on the first page a few manifest blind loyalty, bitter prejudice, or careless superficiality, but the majority of the students
show that they have considered relationship to the church in a
serious way. Few seem to indicate any dogmatic or intolerant attitude. Many apparently have had little acquaintance with modern, progressive churches, and their attitudes are colored by un-
fortunate experiences with conservative and intolerant religious
persons and churches.

Such statements as the following reveal the reason for sharp
criticisms. They show the type of churches that the students have
attended or from which their impressions have come. These statements are given in the students' own words:

> Most churches follow a definite, unchangeable creed which is not prac-
> ticable in the changing age.
> The church is medieval, too slow to keep pace with modern thought.
> The church is hopelessly backward in rational thinking.
> I think most of the church doctrines are absurd and only good for emo-
> tional and ignorant people.
> I have found too much hypocrisy, prejudice, fear of God and hell, and
> too little of human fellowship in the church.

One professor seems to have had only experience of reactionary
groups for he says: "I regard the church as hopelessly allied with
reaction. The leaders are chiefly trained in antiquities. Even if
they have progressive inclinations they shape their teachings to
the more reactionary elements in their congregations." One student frankly confesses: "I am afraid a lack of experience with the
church makes me prejudiced against it."

The students on the average had definite attitudes toward
churches in general and their statements and marking show the
color of their experiences. But many showed that they differen-
tiated between churches and though some of their experiences had

been unhappy ones they had discovered satisfying religiou
groups, practices, and beliefs. One student said: "I have taken a
religious course at the university this quarter and it has mean
more to me than any church in attaining the religious spirit. I
have learned to think of religion in a bigger way than the churche
teach." Another said: "I have been prejudiced against the churcl
by early training but am beginning to have a new value for the
church for I am coming to know different kinds of churches.'
Another said: "I believe the more modern churches are trying to
meet human needs." And a professor confessed: "Toward most
churches I have only a feeling of impatience at their misplaced
emphases and their distorted values, but for such a local church as
the one I attend here I have great admiration because of its con-
structive idealism, though I do not agree with all I hear."

The number of hearty indorsements of the church was rather
surprisingly large and was well distributed among men and
women, and across the different religious groupings, Protestant,
Roman Catholic, and Jewish. Consider the following as frequent
samples:

I thoroughly believe in the church and I think a great effort is being
made to interpret the fundamental principles of religion in the light of our
changing modern life.

I regard the church as the most potent factor in civilization today.

I believe in the church and want to do my part. In spite of its inadequate
adaptation to social conditions I am convinced that it is one of the most con-
structive agencies in society and is in a process of evolution.

The church has had a most important influence in my life. I obtain help
from the church I cannot get elsewhere.

I find my finest friendships in the church.

Of course there were many platitudes and patronizing comments, as:

I think it is a wonderful institution.

I believe the church is a benefit.

I am strongly favorable to the church.

I'm for the church.

It is O.K.
It is a fine thing.

There were a few in each class who showed careless superficiality in their expression of opinion, as such statements as these indicate:

I have never taken church attendance seriously.
I know too little about the church to express an opinion.
I go to church on holidays.
I go to hear special speakers.
I haven't time for the church.
I go to church because I am accustomed to go but I don't know a thing about religion.

A secret longing for greater assurance as to the realities of religion seems to be implied in some of the responses. Some are impatient with the failure of the church to live up to its ideals. Some who have taken religion and the church for granted, without thinking through beliefs and practices, have been challenged for the first time. Consider the following expressions of opinion:

I am confused in my religious ideas but have never had any help from a church. What beliefs I have I've had to work out for myself.
I believe in God but do not find any satisfaction in the church.
I seldom go to church but I pray every day.
I am really religiously inclined but rebel against the narrowness of the church.
I believe in Christianity but it seems to me that denominationalism obscures it.
I believe in Christianity but do not think the church is at all willing to follow the revolutionary teachings of Jesus.
I am a strong evolutionist and can scarcely agree with the church and its doctrines.
I am an atheist but am not against the church.
I do not go to church because the church today seems too far behind the times and too narrow-minded to suit me.
Mere attendance and ceremony mean nothing if a church's teachings are not applicable to daily life in all its phases.
I believe I have to make the best religion I can without the aid of a church.

Although I do not attend church regularly, I believe in a personal God and consider myself religious.

I'd give up the doctrines and creeds of the church for something simple —the symbol of *Good*.

The variety of criticism against the church is interesting. It shows what a difficult task the church has to satisfy all the different kinds of people with different backgrounds, needs, desires, and ideas. Take the following for illustration of student criticism:

Ninety per cent of churchgoers want to be spoon-fed instead of thinking for themselves.

The church is hypocritical, superficial, and meddles in things that do not concern it.

There are too many petty quarrels in the church.

The church is all right, but it could be made a lot more interesting.

It is a waste of time to go to church unless the minister is a man of superior ability.

I have gone to church and Sunday school a lot in my time but have found it unsatisfying and so do not now attend.

The church sanctions un-Christlike activities like war.

The church is a part of the capitalistic scheme to keep people down.

I like the social life of the church but I cannot believe in Christian theology, the divinity of Christ, or a personal God.

I dislike the forms of Christianity. It would be pleasant to believe in some less credulous mysticism.

I am indifferent to the church. Most are social clubs whose members would be horrified if they were required to in any way approximate the revolutionary teachings of their alleged leader. I believe in Christianity but the church is not its representative.

I do not attend church because of the prevalent hand-shaking system.

The foregoing analysis indicates various factors that need attention if the attitudes of an individual or of a group are to be changed. When a series of scales is developed for measuring religious attitudes, they will give valuable information about the attitudes of a group,

The instrument and the methods of its production which we have described offer a pattern for the construction of other scales to measure other religious attitudes. A battery of such tests would serve to give a most worth-while diagnosis of any group with which a religious educator was working and to measure the results of the processes used. Other attitude scales might be developed, such as those relating to the function of the idea of God in the control of conduct; the value of prayer; the observance of Sunday, and the significance of a belief in immortality.

CHAPTER VII

SOME FURTHER PROBLEMS IN THE MEASURE-MENT OF ATTITUDE

AN ALTERNATIVE METHOD OF CONSTRUCTING THE ATTITUDE SCALE

In the present experiment the scale values of the opinions were determined by what we may call the *sorting method*. It is a variation of the method of equal-appearing intervals of psychophysics. Several hundred subjects sort out the statements into eleven piles which seem to them to be equally spaced on a subjective continuum from extreme *pro* to extreme *anti* on the issue in question. This procedure requires the participation of a large group of subjects who during the sorting do not express their own attitudes but merely sort the statements into successive equal-appearing intervals according to the meaning that the statements imply to the readers. Later, when a group is to be studied by means of the scale, the subjects actually vote on the statements in accordance with their own convictions and attitudes.

We shall mention here in passing the possibility of determining the scale-values of the statements without the rather laborious sorting process. It may be possible to scale the statements directly from the voting records of a large group of subjects provided that a considerable range of attitudes is represented in the group of subjects used for this purpose. The principle involved is that if two statements are close together on the scale, then the people who vote for one of them should be quite likely to vote for the other one also. If the statements are very different, spaced far apart on the scale, then those who vote for one of the statements should not be very likely to vote for the other one also.

It might be possible to reverse this reasoning. We might then be able to infer the scale separation between two statements in terms of the number of subjects who indorse both statements, $n_{1.2}$, the number who indorse the first, n_1, and the number who indorse the second, n_2. It is certain that the intrinsic popularity of a statement must be taken into consideration because two statements may belong to the same point on an attitude scale and yet differ widely in the relative frequency with which they are indorsed. This factor of relative popularity is accounted for by the total number of subjects who indorse each statement.

The index of similarity that we have described for the criterion of irrelevance incorporates these three factors in a rather crude way. In a later publication we hope to describe a procedure for scaling opinions directly from the records of voting and, if the procedure shows satisfactory internal consistency of the data, the sorting method here described may be superseded. The sorting method rests on fewer assumptions that can be questioned, as far as we can see now, and it was therefore chosen for our first experiments in the measurement of attitude.

THE VALIDITY OF THE SCALE

The scale must transcend the group measured. One crucial experimental test must be applied to our method of measuring attitudes before it can be accepted as valid. A measuring instrument must not be seriously affected in its measuring function by the object of measurement. To the extent that its measuring function is so affected, the validity of the instrument is impaired or limited. If a yardstick measured differently because of the fact that it was a rug, a picture, or a piece of paper that was being measured, then to that extent the trustworthiness of that yardstick as a measuring device would be impaired. Within the range of objects for which the measuring instrument is intended, its function must be independent of the object of measurement.

We must ascertain similarly the range of applicability of our method of measuring attitude. It will be noticed that the *con-*

struction and the *application* of a scale for measuring attitude are two different tasks. If the scale is to be regarded as valid, the scale values of the statements should not be affected by the opinions of the people who help to construct it. This may turn out to be a severe test in practice, but the scaling method must stand such a test before it can be accepted as being more than a description of the people who construct the scale. At any rate, to the extent that the present method of scale construction is affected by the opinions of the readers who help to sort out the original statements into a scale, to that extent the validity or universality of the scale may be challenged.

Until experimental evidence may be forthcoming on this point, we shall make the assumption that the scale-values of the statements are independent of the attitude distribution of the readers who sort the statements. The assumption is, in other words, that two statements on a prohibition scale will be as easy or as difficult to discriminate for people who are "wet" as for those who are "dry." Given two adjacent statements from such a scale, we assume that the proportion of "wets" who say that statement A is wetter than statement B will be substantially the same as the corresponding proportion for the same statements obtained from a group of "drys." Restating the assumption in still another·way, we are saying that it is just as difficult for a strong militarist as it is for a strong pacifist to tell which of two statements is the more militaristic in attitude. If, say, 85 per cent of the militarists declare statement A to be more militaristic than statement B, then, according to our assumption, substantially the same proportion of pacifists would make the same judgment. If this assumption is correct, then the scale is an instrument independent of the attitude which it is itself intended to measure.

The experimental test for this assumption consists merely in constructing two scales for the same issue with the same set of statements. One of these scales will be constructed on the returns from several hundred readers of militaristic sympathies and the other scale will be constructed with the same statements on the returns from several hundred pacifists. If the scale values of the statements are practically the same in the two scales, then the validity of the method will be pretty well established. It will still be necessary to use opinion scales with some discretion. Queer results might be obtained with the prohibition scale, for example, if it were presented in a country in which prohibition is not an issue.

TWO POSSIBLE TYPES OF ATTITUDE SCALE

The present experiments have been confined to one type of attitude scale. When we started to solve this problem of measuring attitude we found that the scale could logically be constructed along either one of two rather different lines. One of these types was chosen as preferable and the decision was probably correct as far as one can tell as yet. For certain kinds of attitude material it is conceivable that the alternative type of scale would be the preferable.

The two types are illustrated by the two hypothetical diagrams of Figure 24. The upper diagram represents the type of scale with which we have here been working. The ordinates represent the probability of indorsement of a statement while the base line is the scale itself. The interpretation is that any particular statement is most likely to be indorsed by the people who are scaled at the median of the distribution of indorsements for the statement. In other words, as we proceed from one end of the scale to the other by class-intervals, the probability of indorsement for any particular statement increases to a maximum and then decreases again to zero, as shown in the diagram.

Statements differ in intrinsic popularity as shown by the fact that the two hypothetical curves in the upper part of Figure 24 are of unequal area. Even if a statement and a person are scaled at the same point on the scale, it does not therefore follow that the person will necessarily indorse that statement. But when this condition obtains, then the probability is a maximum that the statement will be indorsed. The probability of indorsement of this particular statement is lower for people in other class-intervals than the one in which the statement is allocated. This type of attitude scale may be called the *maximum probability type*.

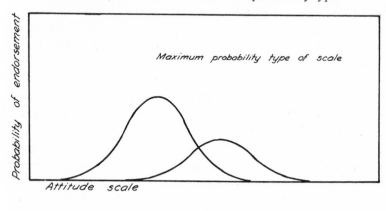

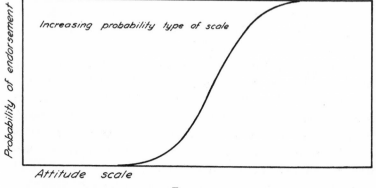

FIG. 24

The alternative form of scale is shown in the hypothetical diagram of the lower part of Figure 20. It is best illustrated by one or two examples. Let us suppose that the issue in question is the desirability of capital punishment. Let the base line represent a series of crimes ranging from minor offenses at the left end of the scale to the most serious crimes imaginable at the right end of the scale. Let us also assume that these crimes have been allocated to the continuum by sorting on the basis of relative seriousness. Now if we asked the subjects to check each crime in the list which they consider serious enough to deserve capital punishment, we should expect to find that as the seriousness of the crime increases the probability of checking for capital punishment would also increase. Very likely the proportion of such judgments would be zero for the minor offenses. It would rise as the seriousness of the offenses rises but there would be no maximum. The curve would be asymptotic probably to the level of unity. If some subjects refuse absolutely to indorse any crimes for capital punishment, then the curve will approach unity but will not reach it. It is also possible that the curve will approach a level below unity. It will not again fall because if the group indorses capital punishment for a crime of a specified degree of seriousness, certainly we expect the same group to indorse capital punishment just as often, or possibly more often, for all crimes that they judge to be more serious. On account of this characteristic we have called this type of scale the *increasing probability type.*

Another example of the same type of scale with a different sort of base line can be thought of for the prohibition question. Suppose that the base line represents the percentage of alcohol that should be allowed. The curve for such a scale would begin supposedly at unity and it would fall toward the base line if the X-scale is one of increasing percentage of alcohol. This is clear because any one who indorses, let us say, 10 per cent of alcohol will almost certainly indorse a lower percentage as legally allowable. The scale-value and the Q-value of a statement so scaled would be determined by methods analogous to those already described.

Still another example of this type of scale would be a list of justifiable provocations for war. Let us suppose that these provocations were listed in rank order of seriousness by the sorting method described. Now if each subject is asked to check those provocations which he considers sufficiently serious or aggravating to justify the declaration of war, then it is reasonable to expect that the person who checks a relatively trivial cause as a suitable provocation for declaring war will also check the more serious situations in the same way. The resulting curve would be a rising probability curve which reminds one of the integral of a frequency distribution which may or may not be normal or symmetrical.

It is possible that certain issues may lend themselves to measurement by the increasing probability type of scale but it is probable that most issues will be better described if the scale is intentionally constructed so that a person is more likely to indorse the opinions at some one part of the scale than at any other part. Such a scale is the maximum probability type.

INDEX

332